Ironstone Whirlygig

Ironstone Whirlygig

Amanda Cook

Bootstrap Press

2018

BOOTSTRAP PRESS

East Coast:

31 Wyman Street
Lowell, MA 01852

West Coast:

1502 Alice Street #8
Oakland, CA 94612

www.bootstrappress.org

ironstone

whirlygig

For the people I love, especially James, Abigail and Sam.
But mostly for my mother and for myself.

TABLE OF CONTENTS

PREFACE

When I started writing *Ironstone Whirlygig*, blogs were all the rage. It started as a sort of open letter to friends, a way to stay in touch. I was working from home for a rare book dealer. Breaks in cataloging were the perfect time to write and respond. The ring of blogs was an early form of social media, a way to connect with friends over the bridge.

As my life changed the blog changed. When Abigail was born time took a different form. Every moment writing was stolen from some other thing that needed doing: laundry, cleaning, cooking, nursing. I wrote mostly about Abigail, about being a mother, about keeping a house.

And then life changed again. My mother was losing her mind. Samuel was born. My days had more in them than I could imagine. I look back at it now as a record of my mother's dementia. If I hadn't written it then I would hardly believe the things that happened. It has become the only history I have of her illness.

I don't know where the years go. My babies have grown. My mother is gone, all but her body. I am running out of people who can tell me my story. I am thankful to have written what I have.

2003

A FTER THE CONVERSATION tonight I wanted to be outside, naked. I put on the kimono a friend's mother made me and went down toward the dock.

I am sure when I do things like this that I won't come back.

I wanted to go to the dock, to be close to the water. I was sure on the way down that I was alone, just like I wanted to be. But as soon as I started down the ramp a door opened somewhere on Cambridge Avenue. A light flickered up near the top of the hill. The tide was going out. Still, there was enough water to swim away if I needed to. But it's the water I am afraid of. For years I have thought that if I should go it would be the water that would take me. I don't want to be afraid of it anymore.

I stood there on the dock for some time, gathering courage. It's not that I am afraid of being naked. I am afraid of being naked alone with the ocean. By this time I am shaking. I don't feel safe. I haven't felt safe for years. I was determined not to give in to it. This summer I will no longer be afraid of the ocean. I will go in on the first count of three. I dropped my kimono and stood there, in the moonlight, for only enough time to know I was there.

MONDAY, JUNE 9

SWIMMING IN LOBSTER Cove for quite some time, skin salty and hair dripping. We went for a little sail in the Babsons' laser, to the end of the cove where the water is warm. The Babson brothers were sitting on rocks looking at birds. Lovely the way water warms on the top and when your feet hang down into the current your toes get so cold. Walk home naked under summer dress, pick peas out of the garden in front of overdressed rich folk walking from their oversized cars to the yacht club for an overpriced dinner. I like to flaunt my bare feet in front of them.

It is nearly morning. At this point I don't see much use in trying to get to sleep. If I wait another hour I can bring the recycling down without waking my grandfather.

The sky was lovely tonight. Sitting on the diving board I saw several shooting stars. No need for wishing, they never come true, but the sight of them...

MY GARDEN LOOKED better with all the weeds in it, but my neighbors will be happier now that all the ragweed is gone. I picked a lemon-yellow tomato today. Ate my first red tomato this morning. Planted some portulaca today; this evening's rain should help it some. My mint is still happy.

My father has some new pain. It worries me. My boss's wife told me my mother came home. I still don't know where she was. My parents make me sad sometimes. Not sad for me, but sad for them. I hope they are okay.

The boys in the kitchen are talking about California and the governor's race. Is it really a better place to live?

I think I am going to bed.

THE MORNING IS muggy as mornings are. Filled with financial planners and watering cans, laundry still to be done and coffee is lukewarm. Wilco on the stereo--thank Mike-o. Gata got tuna this morning, the market is in my future.

Last week my sister said she was a dark cloud hanging over everything. When a dark cloud did roll over us she felt the burden lifted. Alex told me not to get all vesty on him. War sang Low Rider on Regis and Kelly. Dubble Bubble blew LL Cool J away on Today. Rain comes down in sheets and my speedometer is acting up. My mother came back. I figured she would when the sunflowers were big.

My father's anxiety is about breathing, not space, and the wall-oxygen helps. I might have read your poems in Gerrit's birthday box last night. Ken Irby colored pencils! Brenda in pink! Corbett grandchild!

This summer the sun pours down like watered-down orange drink, not honey. Something is always a mess, inside or out. Name dropping could be nothing more than love.

I GATHERED TOMATOES in a long gauze skirt. Yellow and green and red. Cherry and ripe and fallen from the vine. Banished a horned tomato worm. Little, still, but dangerous.

I am caramelizing onions for dinner. Pizza with fresh tomatoes, onions and goat cheese. Salad with garbanzos and tonno in olive oil and fresh herbs.

It is just past seven and I am determined to get something done by eight. This day can't be a complete waste. If it weren't so warm I would make fortune cookies. Speak Chinese. Gray.

MORNING COFFEE BACK to routine 2 with Jim in Lanesville, new boy J.T. Christian, no doubt, and John who mumbles that he hasn't seen me for a long time but I gave him a ride last week from the Lanesville Package Store to Willowrest. Read Rizzo's *Spiritude*, nearly fell off my chair by the time he brought up Moxie what with first and last lines no longer so tied up in each other. At WBZ newstime 8 o'clock I up and go past the guys in front of the Packy up past Judith's house and Ben's and the computer desk on the sidewalk and dill grows out of the crack in the road and everything flowering in the morning mist.

Into my old house with dogs barking and my mother in moon boots I hug her say no to coffee and we start to talk—things are going wrong—I want to tell her not to worry it doesn't matter but it does it all matters. Make a plan when Ralph comes down and talk talk talk like the hum of an old electric typewriter buzzzzz with no pause no space for me to talk and I give up blow up what am I supposed to do? I don't have blinders on.

Drive Mom's car back to her house check engine light on no windshield washer fluid wipers don't even touch the windshield. Call insurance company call Hamer call ophthalmologist call doctor call vet call Robert call everyone for my mother. Kitchen is messy with grime from the stove there is no other word for it but grime black and greasy and everywhere. Push it down deep into my toes get rid of dishpan no sponge wash clean dishes again they aren't clean get rid of dish drain try to clean sink wash dishes again and this time a new load. Clean counter of grime and empty bottles and half-full bottles of every kind of thing like lotion and vodka and orange cleaner and flea soap. Throw it all away.

She gives me money and a heart-shaped rock and chopsticks. I try to refuse it all but no use. Ride home car smells of dog. Stop at estate trash pile to look at stuff what might be a rug is fabric wet fabric she gives me some. I take it home to wash it, nice upholstery fabric but wet. Into the wash as soon as I get home.

Upstairs to rest to work I paint my toenails pink and don't answer the phone toenails wet take a bath bake do laundry. I think I'll take a day off from it tomorrow.

TUESDAY, SEPTEMBER 2

ROUTINE 3: YESTERDAY'S coffee heated up and egg on toast. My new pants are ridiculously long. Iron patchwork from last night and rush out of the house. Woke up too fast still tired but didn't sleep well anyway.

Today she is in her pajamas. Looking through her purse for the accident information, finding everything as if it were new. Trying to explain how she hit the boy's car: monstrous curbs, a loud honk, her turning startled into his car. Can we stop at the insurance place? No. I called them on Tuesday. Won't do any good.

Tired. My eyes hurt. The rain has pooled into a great puddle by Willowrest in the two hours since I was last there. Onto the highway, Hydroplane Lane. She tells the story of the day her mother died and the dog ate the tube of cerulean blue. Sitting on the floor trying to make the puppy vomit. All the dogs at the vet's howling. They are sad because she is sad. And the vet saying "she'll be okay" but no, Marnie's dead. I promise we can buy paint after we buy cleaning supplies.

At the store she buys two of the biggest size of each thing. Does that make the place cleaner? She is drawn to the broken things on the clearance rack. Money in her pocket and still buying broken. I talk her out of it. My boss would say "It's the adult thing to do." Too tired today for this.

Walking in a daze to the craft store, the rain falling harder and harder. Picking up crap and commenting on it. I don't want a blue t-shirt. I don't want a stretch bracelet. I want to go home. I feel myself getting condescending. I don't want to do that. She buys tubes and tubes of paint. I buy yarn I don't need, because I need to do something. I feel selfish with my time. I want to make the trip partly for me.

On the way home I am hungry. I don't want to eat out but I won't have time to stop at home before work, so we stop at the rest stop in Beverly. Sub with vegetables and chicken, not so bad for me. Coffee and muffin for her. Through the purse again and chewing chewing chewing with her mouth open. I am losing patience, if I had any today. More stories, everything always about her. I try to talk. I'm tired. I am just quiet after a while.

In the car on the way home The Connection is on, talking about fonts. My mother is a great sign painter. She has designed several type faces in her day. Today hand lettering is nearly obsolete. She laughs at the names of fonts and recalls her favorites.

At the house I help her bring everything in, unpack the bags. Put the new dish pan and dish drain to use. The black grime is on everything again. It's from the coffee pot, an old percolator. Black from the gas flame. I take time to wash it off, scrubbing years of soot off before going to work. It's the only way. It won't come off my hands and I have to go.

At work now, things not going quite right, and all I want to do is go home and take a bath.

THURSDAY, SEPTEMBER 4

I HAD A horrific Friday and a good and bad Saturday and a lazy Sunday and a decent Monday. Thursday also happened.

High points of the last few days: Patrick and Ariane's party, knitting a ball and a hat, sleeping lots on Saturday, chocolate ice cream and Kahlua, finding the keys I lost months ago in the toy box, devoting Sunday to American football and a bad bad movie, getting email from Simon, getting some good cleaning and reorganizing done, lunch with my Dad (I wish I called him Da... lunch with my Da sounds nice), my cowboy boots coming in the mail and fitting.

Low points of the last few days: My da feeling too sick to stay in Boston for his second appointment, Johnny Cash dying, spilling a bowl of Murphy's Oil Soap on myself, spiders, my mom's breakdown, feeling cruddy cruddy cruddy all weekend, another fish dying.

Some things are getting done, and I like that. Things with me ma are up and down. Today she sounds very together, makes a lot of sense, seems pretty happy, but reports that the clouds in Rockport terrorized her all day. I can understand how they would. I guess that's fine; being sensitive to the atmosphere is better than being miserable.

I bought a ticket to go to Seattle at the beginning of October. Cowboy boots to wear to Seattle!

MONDAY, SEPTEMBER 15

IGNORING ILLNESS WORKING wonders.

The swans in Mill Pond are growing out of their ugly duckling phase. Most of them have shed their brown feathers for pure white but two have gone quite charcoal. Are we set for black swans? I remember one in Cork Loch, seeming to swim against the hundreds of white swans around him.

C AN'T SLEEP, WORRIED about tomorrow. I don't hear the bell buoy but the waves are loud. A light is flickering just enough outside to make my eyes want to be open. It is up near the hill, odd enough, not from the water.

I am thinking of dream places of places to escape and now they are gone to me. Wooded paths I would run down in the moonlight to the water and sometimes in. Crescent beaches where I sat for hours looking for beach glass. The world ignored me in my hours there and then all of a sudden the place was overrun with ghosts.

My mother tells a story about swimming with a seal in Folly Cove. This year she hasn't been in the ocean once. Her eyes don't look out longingly at the water; they are like the water looking carelessly back at the shoreline. I wonder what that seal took from her. What was the trade-off for that swim?

What will I do when tomorrow falls apart? I would like to be able to go back to that beach, take the same path down. Are the ghosts still there? I haven't checked in so long. I am sure the rocks have been moved by storms since then. The ballroom, the split rock, sunset and sunrise. Do urchins still fill that crack? I once found a Christmas tree washed up on the rocks. I stood it up, trunk wedged between two granite boulders. It stayed there for months.

When I was five I walked in my sleep from my room to the antique store my mother owned, just next door and now the bookstore I work at. I curled myself up in a wrought iron crib and slept there until morning. Another time I ended up in the hammock hung between two weeping willows in the back yard. I haven't walked in my sleep since.

I SAW A dragonfly this morning by the back door. He was so large and still there and even when the dog passed his wings barely quivered.

It was a mean mean morning, meaner than I could have guessed, mean enough to almost turn the car around and not go back. Ever. But the afternoon turned to forgiveness and big steps forward. Momentum moves that way as well and let's hope it continues.

Watched the boys do drills on the fields that were once the town dump. The fields are so flat up there but with a little curve to the edges so you think it may be the curve of the earth. The sky raced by with mist hanging and spitting little drops, hair blowing wind-wicked. Just as practice ended the sky opened and as James and I walked to the car we were soaked through. Pools of rain into the cup holders I cleaned with this morning's nervous energy. Glasses wet and not a dry surface to wipe them.

Driving slowly through Main Street currents, water rushing and falling in sheets. Too tired to go home and needing to sit facing each other we ended up at Jalapeño's for soup to warm us and a beer for the long day. Couldn't go straight home anyway. Rain like that floods the corner near Willowrest. Talked and talked. Glad to see Jaime, glad for tortillas, glad to be wet but still not cold. Glad for Chiclets.

On the way home shivering now cold pools easing off the streets and new potholes showing their faces. Up into the tub and into bed and listen to the game phone rings get up write this and though it's early I am going to bed. G'night.

TUESDAY, SEPTEMBER 23

G ERRIT AND I had lunch at Thai Choice. I recommend the Artist's Lunch as a replacement for the Business Lunch. Poets, painters, music makers—go out for lunch! Discuss your ideas and spend time giggling over foolish and important things! Let the gentle pace rule the rest of your day! Then go, if where you are hasn't got good coffee, to someplace that does. Get a pastry. Split it, for goodness sake! What joy is there but in sharing such things!

W E ARE NEARLY rioting here for lack of baseball. The creation of dimples can be a tragic process with long-lasting consequences. That was bloody yesterday.

It is important to note that I bought my cowboy boots before the Red Sox clinched anything. Are you looking for another girl? Pornographic needlepoint can be disappointing and Moomins are hard to find. Little My! I don't want to change the world.

Boston seems so far away some days, what with roads and rain and stomach aches. Noah cleaned my tub on Friday, leaving little footprints of mud. Could've gone to the Pats game today but no! the rain! They've never heard of love.

I can get sentimental when I am homesick. I apologize to all who have been affected. Pears from the back yard make good crisp. They don't know about us.

Berry tea was very berry. Sports can be a good weapon for a girl. Old Joe Clark! Is Arm Sasser because of the catcher? He should know. Josh Reynolds and his stories of Colombian cowboys, holsters and man-purses. I go to the dentist on Thursday.

Melancholy what with having pillows and stuffed mouse thrown at me and still no baseball. Good to be home. Tired, but good.

B AD MOOD DAY. *Later Letters of Lear*, baseball is breaking my heart. Found my own copy of Goops. I knew I knew it from somewhere. Under the piles of art books in other languages. Mom gets art books from the back room, Guest-man Rat balks at the book Rome.

MORNING TALK WITH Gabriel concerning industrialization, then home to clean after being away so much. What evil things lurk in the fridge! Gerrit over for lunch, lovely as always. Me with that feeling, a fluttering in my breast.

Violin in a new spot looking out as far as I can see over the Atlantic. A new piece to learn, with shifts, and a pint for good measure. My mind is wandering and I am letting it go as it pleases. It has nowhere to be for some time yet.

A new song running through my mind so that I have no choice but to listen to it until I know it by heart. Another love song.

THURSDAY, OCTOBER 23

BARELY WAKING, TIME for cleaning. Laundry! Laundry! Special ways for special stains. What in this house can't be vacuumed? Whites in the washer, water the plants.

Some things are lovely enough to note, the way eyelashes cling to each other when wet. How tape laced along the road sparkles in the sunlight.

BEANS FOR CHILI on the stove, tea water on and I am happy for the day. Traffic on the way home from the match was utterly yuppie at the exit for Salem. Witches! Witches! Abigail Faulkner, my great—(add many greats here)—grandmother, found guilty of witchcraft. Erased from public record, "dead" to the public, but not put to death since she was pregnant.

It is nearly the perfect season for naps. Afternoon sun shines into the window by the bed, warming my face. Even though I couldn't sleep I lay there for some time with the orange shine on my eyelids.

SATURDAY, OCTOBER 25

S ITTING NOT QUITE in the dark, not quite in shock, but knowing either is possible.

To Boston with my Da today, hi-diddley-o,
I'll sit and knit in waiting rooms wherever we go.
We'll have fun with oxygen, tanks lined in a row,
to Boston with my Da today! Hi-diddley-o!

THURSDAY, OCTOBER 30

MONDAYS HAVE A habit of feeling just like Monday. Woke up groggy from a weekend of book fairs. Unhappy with the house, not feeling well, no idea how to begin the day. Forget eating, no good food. To market, I decide, but first clean the kitchen.

Dishes books paper yarn. No dry cat food, Gata is mad. Vacuum the floor then mop. Leave it drying with paw prints all around.

Stop on the out to see Charlotte and her new knee. People in my family replace parts. My dad's up for new lungs again, it's got me in a state. I've got his car now and in it I can listen to cd's. Damien Rice makes me melancholy, one song makes me think of someone in particular for no particular reason. To Rowley past sewer work on 133.

At the market I try to use coupons. I stare like an idiot at toothpaste and canned soup and tissues and the like, calculating discounted unit prices. Stopping gray-hair traffic, those ladies can barely push the cart anyway. Give up at the kitty litter, too depressing to eke out the pennies. I'd rather work more. Hard time buying produce with my new rules about the ten most pesticide-ridden fruits and veggies. Leave not sure I have anything I need but still having spent plenty.

At home cook dinner slowly head hurts and body aches. Blacken tomatillos, roast garlic. Chicken in the oven. Rice on the stove. Puree tomatillos with chipotles and cilantro. Tortillas warming. Roast summer squash and zucchini. Re-fry beans.

James gone now, I stay home. Trying to get better so I can see my da tomorrow. Bringing him lunch. Want to spend some time.

I don't think I have crushes this week. I have worries and cares. Some nice thoughts of people in particular and some guilt for missing readings. Happy to have made guest appearances in dreams but unhappy with the dreams I am having. Add them to my list of worries.

C UTTING ONIONS FOR chowder the blade of the knife comes free and stays fast in the onion. No thyme but bay leaves. Salvaged two potatoes from the cupboard, should have had three. Fish stock in the pot and in a bit haddock.

RIED GETTING UP on both sides of the bed today, hoping one would be right. No luck. Morning phone call from my ma. Tried to reassure her but I really have no idea. The wind is whistling outside, Gata meowing in, and me grumping about all of it.

What is fair and what isn't? If it weren't so cold and windy I would throw all the windows open and clear this house out. The air needs some clearing. I could drink a lot of water. Cancel credit cards. Wash clothes. Nothing will be fixed by it, trust me. An article I saw yesterday had firemen and businessmen and little girls meditating.

To keep the cat from attacking the printer I have closed her out of this room. The fish tank needs filling, its gurgle is distracting. Wind on the left, water on the right.

THURSDAY, NOVEMBER 13

T HERE ARE HURTS that don't go away. They follow us like the dead or the lost, and we mourn them as such.

PULLED DEAD SUNFLOWERS out of the garden this morning. Picked an onion. Splinter in my finger, removed but with a slight wound in its place. Trying to put order into the week, the week into order, a weak order, really. Time is filling up. How can I let YOU down?

THE SPLINTER I took out of my finger yesterday left a big hole. A big hole that hurts. It interferes with my bow hold and my knitting. It hurts when I do dishes. It hurts me so.

Friday my grandmother from Hawaii flies in. I am picking her up at the airport and will miss Mark's reading. Her coming makes me nervous about my father. She is feeble herself and it makes me wonder just how bad he is if she is coming out on such short notice. But I miss her and love her and look forward to sharing a bottle of wine with her. I wonder how long she is staying.

A friend's grandfather died last week. He was a great man and will be missed. Friend says he just got weaker and weaker then died. Bodies do that, I guess, just give up.

HOME TO A dark house smelling of smoke and the house matching my smell but its smoke of wood, mine of stale bar. Songs on the radio on the way home. You and me babe, how about it.

My mind spins when it is windy and warm. Along the causeway they are building a walkway named after a friend of mine killed there. It will interfere with one of my favorite morning views, sort of like the suicide fence on the A. Piatt Andrew. I hope this is more successful.

Met a man in the bar tonight who remembered my aunt Judy. He deaf across the bar, raising his glass and I raising mine, to Judy. When I was 16 and ready to escape Gloucester and the way it had trapped me Judy was sailing in the Pilot from Gloucester to California, through the Panama Canal with her husband Ross. I spent some time with them and the rest of the crew on the boat as it was docked near the state fish pier. A boy on board not too much older than I was at the time gave me a sprig of sea lavender he had gathered somewhere on a previous sail. I still have it in one of my many little wooden boxes. Long after Judy died, long after my first sailing adventure. Long after her brother and I cried, drunk, in the cabin of his Mug Up in Belfast Harbor, singing songs to Judy.

I T'S SORT OF a lonely morning, dreary and rainy. A horrible day for a funeral. After dropping James off and driving Alex to school I wanted to be around people. Bar people. I wish I knew where the Crow's Nest people are at eight in the morning. I probably should have checked the Crow's Nest.

Drove through Manchester hoping to stop for coffee. Everything looked too just-so for me. Continued on to Caffé Sicilia. An hour later than usual, all the spots at the tables near the front were taken. I ended up at the table near the door and with no knitting and nothing to read. I sat there, alone. Left lonely still. Considered going to Trupiano's for meat for stew. Changed my mind and headed home in a round-about way through Rockport.

Went to the hardware store to wait for the yarn store to open. Considered light bulbs, paint, hardware for shelving. I should have measured something before I went. I could have measured anything. I ended up buying a little chopper that was on sale to replace my mini-Cuisinart that died during Christmas candy making last year.

With my new chopper's help I talked myself out of yarn. Went to IGA instead. Lots of root vegetables for stew. Home through Lanesville, one last chance to end the loneliness of the day. Postcard stamps from Lenny at the post office. Into the café where a new girl was working and the old postman who was arrested a couple years back was there talking to her. He makes me uncomfortable. No comfy coffee time for me, I left soon after I got there. To the package store, a bottle of burgundy for the stew and cabernet for drinking.

Browned the meat, turning first with chopsticks then a metal spatula. I hate using metal utensils, prefer wood, but with flour sticking to the pan and meat sticking with it I gave in. Onions and celery and carrots into the pot, just a couple minutes until the onions are soft. Meat back in, bay leaves, salt and pepper, cover it over with wine and a little broth. Amused by the new appliance. Chop mushrooms until they are barely mushrooms at all, sauté them, toss them into the pot. Using finely chopped vegetables for thickening.

Waiting now for the meat to turn fork-tender. Bowls of hand-cut root vegetables are on the table, waiting to go in. Turnips, potatoes, carrots and parsnips. Those little boiling onions. Maybe more mushrooms, halved or quartered. Cutting by hand is ultimately more satisfying. Toss some rosemary in on a whim.

Don't know what to wear to the service. Should I walk to the church? If I can find my umbrella. Not lonely anymore, it doesn't take much for me. Just a comfortable feeling.

SATURDAY, NOVEMBER 22

MY MOM FOLLOWED me to work today. She came in through the house not the office and talked to me there in the kitchen. I couldn't keep myself from looking at the triptych of G mowing around Galen's grave. Galen's grave. I don't go there as much as I should or as much as I want to, just down the street but I haven't felt safe there for years. Always looking over my shoulder. We used to ride bikes there, the lot of us, but it is filling in now with graves. Galen then Will then Norma and who else? I haven't been, I don't know. And it is December now. I would leave the country if I could.

THE SNOW IS piling up out there. After nearly denouncing Christmas my grandfather got a tree and began to decorate. While I was at the hardware store getting new fuses for his light the electricity went out. Armed with a flashlight from their emergency kit I found them anyway. Got out by pulling the usually-automatic doors apart.

Can't find some books at work that are in the next catalog. Don't know who is supposed to plow there but I had to leave before I was snowed in. Received an order from a man named Snow.

James says we should cut down the tree across the way for Christmas. I assure him it would be noticed. Last spring the neighbor asked my grandfather if he could cut it down to improve their view. He said no and in that instant, thinking that maybe he wasn't being such a nice neighbor, told him that it was my grandmother's favorite tree. I assure you it wasn't.

I wish the leftovers in my fridge were gone. I would like to cook some nice new food but don't think I can because to waste food is bad. They aren't even my leftovers, most of them. I want to make a big pot of spinach oatmeal soup.

I have a hard time saying I am fine lately, even if it is true. Such a delicate balance. So many things could go wrong I feel like I should at least be prepared. That seems better than being very very happy and being blindsided.

SATURDAY, DECEMBER 6

I T'S HARD TO be this vulnerable. I spend my time pretending poems are written for me even when I know they aren't. So what if my name isn't Maria? My name could always be Maria.

I volunteer to teach Xtina about sports for when she marries that Harvard meathead. As with most things it is a matter of language and logic. Learn the language first. "Pooch kick" the ball, down it at the one-yard line. Run the clock down. It's as easy as pie. I also volunteered to teach Xtina how to bake pie.

It is important to note here that Xtina is not marrying a Harvard meathead anymore than the poems I have been reading are about me. If she were to do so, however, her being a master of language and logic would certainly help her understand sports.

James says this sounds mean. I certainly don't mean it to be. If anything I am looking to convert another girl to the world of football. And baseball. And real football. Or just to hang out with Xtina more.

LAST NIGHT IN my dream there was a new kind of Moxie, Alpine White. Black Arthur was selling it in a little stand maybe a hundred yards past the last entrance to the Seaside Cemetery. The Gibsons were sitting on the old rock. I was bleeding.

Earlier this week I dreamed we were fishing. Not really. We were standing on the beach, but one or two people were in the water. Some large fish were swimming in toward shore, chasing smaller fish in toward the shore. I'm not sure what the smallest kind was, then pogies, then blue fish. I am deathly afraid of bluefish and was very nervous for whomever was treading water, mostly for the safety of their toes. The fish were jumping onto the beach and because it seemed like there was no other appropriate thing to do we were gathering them.

My sister gave birth on Thursday to her fifth boy. I took the other four, from 18 months to 7 years of age. Early in the morning on Thursday until a little past noon on Friday. They wore me out and I am coming down with a cold. Elijah (the youngest) moves things. Bath salts are now in the bedroom. A bowl of fruit loops in the hall. Playmobil everywhere. I found a pair of socks stuffed under the heater in the bedroom this morning. I will be finding things for some time to come.

I have been so tired lately, too tired even to knit. This is no good what with Christmas coming and so many things left to make. I am thinking that Christmas presents will turn into Groundhog Day presents or Valentine's Day presents. Maybe I'll just wait for the Epiphany. My intentions are good but really I am worn out.

SATURDAY, DECEMBER 20

2004

G OOD NEW YEAR and a sleepy day—lovely party yesterday, I like to have you in my home. Things are decided in an arbitrary way when the year changes. I am as guilty of this as the next fellow but am too tired to talk about it.

Maybe tomorrow.

T WO DAYS AGO the water between here and the beach had iced over completely. Now that the temperature has risen water is flowing through the channel, bringing chunks of ice with it. My little cove is still all ice. It is trapping other floes along its edge.

I guess I am well-rested but I lack any momentum. I make little lists in my head of little things I could do then I don't do them. I'll have to get up and do something soon but today is a holiday and that's reason enough for me to do nothing.

Tomorrow. Tomorrow I will do something.

OVER THE BRIDGE and out of town route 128 route 114 route 1 and 62. Fabric store and market and flower store then lunch. Philodendron gardenia dwarf orange hibiscus jasmine. Lamb change mind beef in the pot and mushrooms and onions and Guinness three Guinness. Boil boil boil. Too tired to finish wait to cool cook more in the morning and maybe chocolate bread pudding. Too hard on myself too tired this should pass soon sitting waiting for stew to cool glass shelves and room in the fridge. Someone on my mind someone always on my mind my mind always on someone and a new picture of my da and me got it this morning from my stepmother me young him young and not even any tubes.

ICE FLOES CREPT over the edge of the pier this morning, stacks of packed ice. I looked for seals.

Lunch with my mother today. First time since my father's passing, first time we've talked. Looking out over Rockport water changing color: cerulean blue and cadmium red and cadmium yellow... now add fuschia. Now no yellow. Her first onion ring in years; get rid of the small fears and work on the big ones. Talk a lot, cry just a little, more together than I'd expected.

To violin with coffee and cookies for a quick tune-up. Pegs keep slipping. Over-attentive parents of the next student offering advice for cheering up. I could play duets with their ten-year-old daughter. Take b vitamins. Long walks. They don't know what's going on and nobody tells them.

HOME TONIGHT, NOAH'S over. Lots of confusion over death and dads. Who is my father now? When Luke Skywalker's father dies Darth Vader became his father and then Darth Vader became a good guy and then he died too. If mom and dad die, we'll take care of you. If I die I promise to call your mom so she can come get you first. My father is still my father and is still Noah's grandfather. He's with us in spirit, like Yoda and Old Ben. But not in blue. That's in spirit in *Star Wars*.

TUESDAY, JANUARY 27

COLD AND BROKEN as the day. Tiny snow crystals dancing around outside the window, occasional birds and cars passing by. The views keep changing. My mother hasn't come to see me today. A little lonely, wish I were busy, wish it were warm enough to want to do anything. Just an hour left before I can go home. Dishes to do there, maybe a warm bath, a chance to just be home.

LITTLE HEART BEATING double-time, swifter than I imagined. Mind wanders. Always wandering sometimes lost. On whom? Whomever!

I N THE WORST mood today for no apparent reason. I think it's getting better. Wrapped books for four hours. Watched a stupid movie. That helped. Maybe a warm bath next.

I realized last night that I have started giving canned answers sometimes when people ask about my father. I am sorry for that. Sometimes it is easier than actually thinking about it. That's why Hallmark makes cards, so we don't have to think about things too much. Jack's first poem nearly killed me with the air in the lungs and all. Took things back out of catch phrases.

Gata has been stalking me whenever I am home. She wants me in bed at all times so she can curl up around my legs. I suppose that's what we all really want anyway.

WASHED THE LEAVES of the plant that has been next to my bed for years. Moved it to the top of the bookcase where the long-dead goldfish plant was. Moved the miniature orange tree to the window where the first plant was.

The car has gone from grumbling to grinding to klink-klanking. Tomorrow she goes in. We'll see if she comes out.

Mary Cassat and candy heart stamps. Talking about the mean postman with Lenny and Rob. His life must be bad. To be so mean.

Finished the book I was reading and it's too bad there isn't more.

Spring catalogs are easy to recycle these days. Nothing fits me and nothing will fit me for some time.

S OAKING SMALL WHITE beans overnight. For baked beans tomorrow. To eat with Fenway Franks, in celebration of the new year.

TRYING NOT TO be so silent. This little thing in my belly is taking most of my mind. Blood meant for my brain ends up in my uterus and I'm left stuttering for hours on end.

It feels like spring here. May be time to leave our shells. Walked along Halibut Point Sunday afternoon, mud and rocks and a few moments so close to the surf I had to reach down and taste the water carried in. That side of the Cape is freshest to me, more Atlantic than Bay. I spent my childhood swimming less than a mile away at the Flat Rocks, crawling into granite caves and gathering sea glass.

TUESDAY, MARCH 2

STAYED OUT TOO late three nights in a row, spent the day trying to make it up to my body but couldn't find a way to get comfortable. Tried napping but the music is too loud shut the door and just when eyes agree to stay closed wake to the sound of furniture being thrown off the front porch. The round wooden table I have eaten at since I was a child and the metal couch I had helped my grandmother cover with blue vinyl to withstand the weather, the perfect place for an outdoor nap in the sun. Both thrown off the porch and broken before being sent away and all I can think of as I am listening is my aunt a few weeks before she died sitting in the sun on the porch eyes almost vacant but still some light and her little girl barely a year old playing on the same furniture I played on.

Why do this? Why break things? Can't we just leave them be until the time comes to leave them behind?

FINISHING JARS OF jellies and jams. Rose petal and quince, beach plum. Ginger, gooseberry, apricot and orange still too full to consider. Wash the linens and pack them away, tablecloths embroidered with the initials of Faulkners long gone.

Talked to the man who will sell me insurance for our house. Seems he used to own it. Talked about used books and NPR, book dealers selling online. He reads science fiction and orders British authors from a man in Canada before they are published here. He is happy we don't have a dog or a trampoline.

Work today, new catalog out. Body feels wrecked, back and hips. I swear I will be in better shape before I do this again. This winter's stress and sorrow must have taken its toll. Strengthen and stretch to baseball, music and reading. Must not sway my back.

RAIN DELAYS ARE no good for me. I saw Fuddruckers on the Phanton Gourmet and got to thinking about my father. One of the last times we went to Boston together for appointments we stopped on Route 1. He couldn't eat his whole burger but we had a good time. Cleaning yesterday I found a letter I wrote to my father while he was still in isolation after his lung transplant, me sitting at Fuddrucker's on the way home from the hospital because I wanted to be somewhere he enjoyed.

Saw the hot peppers on the condiment bar on the television and it got me to thinking about how much my father enjoyed little things in this world. I realized how much pain he must have been in to decide to die and how long he must have been in pain.

So I start crying and I leave the room. Come in here and try to get things off my mind by checking who was voted off American Idol. Give me baseball or give me fluff. Without whiskey it is the only way I will make it through.

FRIDAY, APRIL 30

INSTRUCTIONS FOR TODAY:

Take one lilac blossom from a bunch.

Place the blossom in between your lips, crown facing out.

Gently breathe in the nectar.

SATURDAY, MAY 15

RAIN, RAIN, GO away. At the beginning of the week I was happy for the rain, for its watering my garden. Now my lettuce looks like it could use a little sun.

I could too.

L ISTENING TO BALLADS that bring me to tears.

Gerrit and Elijah and I off to lunch today then at the cafe, with Gerrit playing peek-a-boo behind the neon signs and he says something about the people we can never introduce.

I'm bound for the waves, and rain comes in a serpent-cloud over the harbor. In the car home a Kinks song covered by Kirsty MacColl makes me cry. Predictable, really, but still. Bits of sun fighting to shine on the Annisquam. My peas haven't come up yet and my baby will never meet my father.

Then doing dishes just now—this cruel country has driven me down. I've only sad stories... my dreams have withered and died. Thinking of friends who hurt each other and jealousy and love. They'd run and hide. Sad but with sorrow, not depression. And when those you love hurt each other, silver moon sailor, silver moon shine. Last night's moon the strawberry moon—if I were a butterfly I'd live for a day. My dreams have withered and died.

Baby kicked hard while I was in the tub tonight, hard enough to see my belly move. To Canaan's Land, I sang at my grandmother's service. At a friend's grandfather's funeral old people I can't name asking me to sing when they die. And how time passes—a love-light shines across the sea and the soul of man never dies.

My grandmother always with something red about her and drinking

Manhattans. Elijah so dear to me and conceived barely a month after she died. Elijah the same age as the second baby I lost would be and so dear to me, whistles between his teeth sometimes when he breathes and blows kisses. My heart it bleeds, for she loves him indeed. Sing hi-ho-lay at the end of the day. Elijah who calls "manna's home" when I arrive and who is so dear. Let the years come and go.

The song that made me think of Marnie but now I think Judy and little Emily who isn't so wee any more. Who now will sing me lullabies? Listening to it in the barn playing pool with my sister and Noah then three starts to cry because the song sounds so sad and Elizabeth and I can't not cry. The stars are all fading and Emily in California never got her lullabies.

Some tyrant has stolen my true love away. William and Davey, come round here no more—wed I am oh and happy I shall be. Rise my love and go away. I wish to God I'd gone before you.

The good ship sails on the ally-ally-oh.

READING SHORT STORIES this morning. All of them are about love, and none of them are happy. There is just the moment. If I cut my hair short it won't hang down over my breasts in the moonlight. One ends with horses, another with going away.

Thursday was for parents and Friday for grandparents. Today is for me and I must dress well. There will be disappointments, there always are. I would like to unwrap hours and give them to people to spend with me. I would like a quiet day. My mind and body are tired.

I will be happy with women I know who love me. I will be grateful for the help and gifts they give. I will write thank-you notes. I will mean it. But I will be wanting to be quiet with somebody—the baby in my belly or a warm body in my bed.

Tomorrow is pomp and circumstance. Sit in the stands, be together. James and Samantha on the field for different reasons, a lei for Sam and one for my father's grave. Collapsing I'm sure by the end of the day to do the work I should be doing now.

This next week quieter than the one before it, Simon gone and others resting. If I could fill in some of the time the same way. I will get my hair cut. I am not sure how. Noah's haircut is wonderful and he looks so much like I looked at five. But it is short and might not do.

Into the tub now and to get ready. My toenails are chipped and should be painted but I can barely reach them. I have a birthday outfit to wear if it fits me and a smile to paint on. I should be prepared.

S UNBURNED FROM GRADUATION. Right arm lobster-red, left arm protected by a sleeping baby. My chest in the deep v of a new halter dress. Cheeks and nose and forehead. I haven't been burnt like this in years. Seven years today, when the scalloped neck of my wedding gown was burnt into my breast.

Not a word about my mother missing my shower. For years she fought tooth and nail to claim the role of parent and now not even a façade. She has no problem with my stepmother taking over the public role. Maybe she gave up the fight. Maybe the fight was never over us.

Sunday idyllic looking out on the Canal at Newell Stadium. Boats going by and the field filled with kids in maroon and white, my half-sister among them. James there on the field watching his students and handing Samantha her diploma. She wore the pink lei, put on her by my nephew as I sat in the stands with my grandmother BJ and the rest of the kids.

Tuberose flowers falling off of the other, too much for a girl trying to fit in. The woman behind us remembers the smell of the airport in Honolulu. My grandmother says tub-e-rose where I pronounce it tube-rose. I will change my way. Fallen flowers in the buttonholes of my cardigan. Caleb crying on my shoulder from the noise of the band but sung quickly to sleep. Lovesick ballads again.

Bring the baby back to my sister. Look down—no wedding ring on my stepmother's finger. Speeches about childhood and movies. I hope you dance. Names and names and names, proud parents with noisemakers and cowbells. Fighting our way onto the field to find Samantha and James. BJ hobbling down eventually, by then me collapsed in a city councilor's chair. Pictures and congratulations.

At home tired from the heat and sun, skin aching against the sheets. Aloe sinking in slowly. Cool breeze from the water making me shiver. Asleep by the third inning.

T O DO LIST, June 16:

- buy liver
- buy soap
- get letter from lover
- visit newspaper
- attend funeral
- go to prostitute
- masturbate on beach
- eat gorgonzola sandwich

TUESDAY, JUNE 15

I DIDN'T GET the love notes I was hoping for. I can bring myself near to tears with anticipation, foolish anticipation.

In some ways I got more.

My list was a bust. I can't eat gorgonzola while pregnant and really I have no idea how to find a prostitute. Didn't make it to the beach. I did visit the newspaper but that's it. I didn't even buy soap.

There is a general feeling of uneasiness around me. In some cases it leans toward bitterness, in others hopelessness, and in me I can't figure it out. I spend hours imagining what could happen, hours talking myself out of or in to what I have imagined, and hours cursing myself for hours wasted. Right now I am waiting for water to boil, which means these moments can't be considered among them.

I have left helplessness out of the uneasiness. Please forgive the mistake.

Molly Bloom and the baby she lost, shouldn't have buried him in the sweater she knit but what else could she do? I have a sweater started for my last and I can't bring myself to finish it for Whomever. Can't bring myself to take it apart. My grandmother here remembering her lost child, her youngest, named James. Two sons gone and she is left to her wine bottles. Now when she counts her children I don't know what the number is.

My stomach is upset, it might be affected. Some things I wish I didn't know and I know it is better I do. The truths we know but can no longer deny once given the facts. The truth being variable and the facts constant. The chart Gerrit made me is hanging by a clothespin above the computer. It reminds me of parts of myself.

My body has never been a teenage body and never will be. I can't say why this matters but as I get closer to being a mother it feels like I am fulfilling some kind of prophecy. The decision was made by my hips and breasts before they knew to show themselves. My body is heavy and will always be heavy. My troubled mind is in my bosom and womb and I can't seem to get my arms around it. My body feels like the vessel it is and I can't make it feel any different.

COFFEE WITH MY mother, sister and some of the boys, sunny table at The Market and everything seemed good. Kenny H. had a good joke about my grandfather's cliff driving—"they didn't have air brakes?" Just heard on the radio that an accordion festival will hit Boston next month.

Saturday night I should have been drunk given the occasion of afternoon football at the Kinvara, but baby says no. Kicks so much it must be a striker. Dino looking good for not smoking. I miss the lads. By the time the Celtic season starts I should have a wee one at my breast.

To the 108 with treats for Lucy, Thai food from across the street and a dress that didn't do too well containing me. The music was nice but I would have preferred no horn—too close to the voice sometimes. I wish Joe was there. I have words for him that don't make it into email. I wish I saw John more.

Baby keeps me from sitting still too long, chair then floor and stretch this way and that. I wish I could have softened some of the sounds for my womb, thinking of Lucy and Anders and Caleb all overwhelmed by noise.

If Mike County were a plant he would be lamb's ear, planted in the shade of a rosemary bush in the front garden of a row house in the southern outskirts of Cork.

Jim Dunn read about the beach in Magnolia. I spent the summers of fourteen and fifteen drinking at bonfires there while my stepmother played oblivious a hundred yards away. Cheap beer with fraternal twins twice my age. One I wanted to kiss. The other declared one night sitting on the stone wall next to the local garage that if the world were to end tomorrow he would take me up in his arms and not let go. Saw him years later at Pavilion Beach watching the greasy pole, still drunk. His brother was the one who told me my horn was going off at Friendly's a couple years ago.

Breakfast at The Dory yesterday. The guy who walked the pole dressed as a jester at the table in back, telling the story of Andy who fell off the wagon and hasn't been seen since. Didn't even swim in with the rest of the walkers. Swam to the boats instead, leaving his girlfriend waiting on the beach. Heard he's alive but he still hasn't made it home. Then the boy who won on Friday and Saturday comes in. The waitress was hoping he'd win all three days. He's no Jake Wood. No Peter "Black" Frontiero.

Henry Ferrini in with big news about his film and his son holding a stuffed animal and a spatula. Turn around in the lot looking into the harbor. Remains of Fiesta still in St. Peter's Square, carnival truck and tinsel angels. Scaffolding bones of the altar. I'd challenge that guy who said the Fort was gentrified to carry Peter through the streets and watch the women throw confetti from the windows. There have always been a few outsiders living there but let's make it clear: Olson wasn't a fisherman either.

The sailors weren't as good looking this year. Might be because I wasn't drunk. More so I think it's the war. Walking the streets with James, talking to former students, now enlisted men, trying to keep themselves out of Iraq and Afghanistan. Little boys still, not more than babies, looking for ways to stay safe. And Dan home on leave, a few more weeks left in which he can be sent away, all our fingers crossed and we pray even if we don't believe.

I should pack more now. I've killed the difficult plants and won't have to move them. I should never be trusted with jasmine or gardenia. The hibiscus by my bed hasn't got the weight to handle the sea breeze and I haven't the heart to close the window. Yesterday its three blossoms were overshadowed by the lilies from Greg, standing tall in their milk-bottle vase. Perfect backdrop for my reading *Women Poets of China*. Fragrant flowers near the cool sheets of my bed.

Tuesday, June 29

AWESTRUCK BY THE beauty of the world today. The red of a barn between 133 and exit 13, the orange and yellow of lillies by the road. Blue sky turning gray then white then blue. I am not as overwhelmed as I could or should be, but I am sure that will pass.

Emptying drawers for the move, room by room. This should all be done by now. The heat is getting to me. Packing nearly naked, and it isn't even that hot. Unaccustomed to corners without clutter, embarrassed by how many things I have. Books, yarn, clothes, shoes. Dishes and pans and pots and fabric. Records and books and books and books.

THURSDAY, JULY 15

SLEPT IN THE new house last night—mattress on floor, box spring too wide for the stairs. Gata howling on the way over but content after a few minutes of cuddling. Not too hot with the fan going, bed made like home because it is home now.

Book cases in the study, quick visit from Lansing etc. while I took my first shower. So much to do and so much done. So many thanks that need be given. Thank you for your help. A little overwhelmed still, made it through only crying once this morning and that was after slamming my finger in the door.

James took the tape off of the edges in the living room. The couch is set against the left wall, the computer as well for now. Mountains of white bags in the living and laundry rooms. Two loads of laundry done, fridge moved a little, shower curtain up. So tired today and trying not to do too much, a day of rest. Nothing to eat in the house and I'm not going shopping.

Let the fish go this afternoon in my brother's fish pond. After looking lost for a moment he started to swim with the big fish, following their circles around the lazy brown school near the deepest part. I wonder if he will be so pale next time I look. The orange fish in the pond are so bright, the white shimmer, the brown sulk. My pale little fish stands out.

Gata likes the back of the couch for sleeping. I might try to rest in a bit.

Spent some time at River Rd., mostly talking to my grandfather. Cleaned a little and left James packing more. Someone is coming to look at the house on Tuesday or Wednesday, hopefully the latter. Our place is a mess but Hamer isn't worried. I won't worry either. Tomorrow I will go and try to make some order of it. Today it is too much.

T IRED FROM THE heat. Rooms are cool at certain times, lights off and fans going. Drink water. Drink water. Always boxes on the living room floor, always new boxes to replace those we have emptied.

Gata sleeping mostly on the floor, water in the bedroom window by the street. A strange mark with no fur near her nose, no idea how it got there. She doesn't seem to mind it. This window as good as the last and closer to the action.

Dinner at the Douds' last night, the boys talk about Leonard Cohen and those lines from "Sisters of Mercy" stick in my head. We weren't lovers like that and besides it would still be alright. Girls into one room, boys in another, talking and talking. Pavement in the kitchen.

Went to Trader Joe's today with my sister and two boys. One left here with James and two more playing elsewhere. Food in the freezer for now or later. Tomorrow maybe Farmer John's for fruits and veggies. Kitchen stuff still unpacked and I have no idea where to put it. Need a curtain for the window upstairs, may take out my sewing machine this evening. Tired of not being able to do and tired of asking.

Baby kicking something crazy today. Belly moves as whomever shifts and I feel my insides pushed around. When will the heat break? Shoes didn't fit this morning and I don't know where the rest are. Bags of sweaters upstairs, I can put them away. Laundry has a place to go once it is folded. Should I wash the sheets tonight or wait? May go to bed very early...

Hoping for thunder.

HIPS ARE SORE in the morning, the weight of the womb and all. The sun wakes me long before the bus honks outside for Eric, the boy in our backyard. Took a bath into a shower and back into bed. Why can't I stay naked in bed all day? For modest visitors I would pull the covers up to my chin. Getting dressed is such a hassle these days.

Gerrit arrives for coffee and Portuguese sweet bread, new corn broom in hand for the new house. Gooseberry jam and Xtina's condiments. Gata wants out the back door, asks politely with one paw raised. I still say no. Bag of baby clothes left on the back porch, no note, but twelve months written in a hand I recognize.

Nap time, morning nap, Gata with paws crossed over my hand as I sleep. One hour of sleeping and one hour of thinking. Thinking of you, of all of you. I am starting to say sentimental things and I hope you don't mind.

Sent home last night with leftover turkey, open-faced sandwiches for lunch. No cranberries but dried, thrown in a pan with some orange juice then zzzed. New table in the kitchen, old diner table kept for years in my father's basement, moved from James's grandparent's house. A better shape for facing each other. Wooden table into the study.

Off now to the old house, to get plants and cinderblocks and wood for building shelves. Mirror and the wedding present from Chris. Painting of me at age five riding the carousel at St. Peter's Fiesta, wearing my favorite dress. Maybe the antique cradle. Medium dishes for serving sweet bread toast to your favorite people.

MONDAY MORNING. DID the dishes, swept the floor, nearly done with the laundry. I never thought I would enjoy laundry this much.

Watching movies lately, what else to do at nine months? The rumor that I don't like movies is not true. I just like to watch them at home where I can do something useful at the same time. Or at Gerrit's, where he treats me like a princess.

Odd couple of days there, Friday and Saturday. Down, not out, but down and not happy about it. Family information I am uncomfortable knowing. Makes me think in a way I don't like to think. Friday baby slow to move, or just sleepy, who knows. But enough of a change to make me worry. Might have been me doing too much and not taking the time to feel little kicks and nudges. Could be because it is a little more cramped in there than before. Saturday spent being more still, eating more regularly. Kicks back to normal. Friendly faces in the afternoon and evening. Mystic Pizza. Irby's lemon tart. Tea in a big cup.

My grandfather finally opened the pool, no locust trees this year and even no chairs. But I can go and pack more junk, swim. Remember mermaid days. Skin sliding through the water, light and music from the barn as friends shoot pool. Night swimming, naked, when the air is as cool as the water. Swimming until teeth chatter and limbs are useless, finding my way inside, sleeping with the moon in the window and off the water.

INSTEAD OF NAPPING when I should have I read a book. Now I feel flustered like I often do after reading a book in one sitting, unable to separate the book from myself or my thoughts from the book. The boy in the book was afraid of things he didn't have a system for. I am afraid of things I don't have a system for.

Driving home in the rain my stomach hurt. It hurt on and off while I was reading and my lower back too but in no pattern. I was lying down and it is hard for me to tell sometimes when I am lying down because my hips can hurt as well. Now I am sitting up and I feel fine. Better, at least.

I am unsettled by never having done this before. And by the fact that there is no pattern to follow, no right way. My uterus contracts. I feel pain. Nothing happens for hours or days. My back hurts and this is normal. And it could mean nothing. I am afraid the book had something to do with this—I was not unsettled before. Unsure, yes, uncertain, of course, but not unsettled.

It is my mother's birthday. She thought I would have the baby today. She is bucking the system and thinks it is a boy. Because I have an innie. It would have to be an incredibly short labor to make today the day. I have been counting on a longer prelabor to tie up loose ends. I think I will tie them up now. Maybe then I won't feel unsettled. But I don't just want to wait. Having things undone means I am not just waiting. My head is woozy, I am going now. To get something to drink. And tie up loose ends.

SATURDAY, AUGUST 21

ONE WEEK OLD. I don't know what to say. Waking up to see that she is breathing, singing to her wrapped in my arms. New sleep patterns, new ways for everything. Watching her eyes lighten from steel gray to blue. Changing her and dressing her and taking good care. Friends stop by with love and fruit. Holding her close, as close as I can.

FINDING BOTH MY hands free for the first time in weeks, dinner done and waiting and Baby Girl on her daddy's shoulder. Nurse nurse nurse, my daily routine. Little bits of doing things in between. Mostly laundry, mostly diapers, an occasional walk. She sleeps well most nights and I sleep.

Wrote that last night, the time was short-lived. Right now the baby is sleeping and that worries me. If she is sleeping now will she sleep later? If she doesn't sleep later when will I sleep? Strike that, little sounds of waking are coming from where she lies. Some like stretching, some like cooing, some about to be upset that I am not changing or feeding her.

Before I need to go I should say that I read your email and will write back soon, I hope. I look forward to seeing you, hopefully I will make it, but it is too early to promise. It all depends on the baby girl.

TUESDAY, SEPTEMBER 14

SUNDAY ONE DAY after one month. These moments are hard to find and I should be doing more with them—laundry, dishes, find my clothes. One thing I know to be true: these things will still need to be done. They will not go away.

I bought a camera yesterday and have been wasting time with it since. Pictures of the baby girl. She's eating her fingers like they're just another meal.

FEELING A LITTLE disoriented, maybe alienated. Looked online to find my friends but I can't remember which go where. Looked for Pedro's midget, knit Ugg boots, a place to fit in. My arms are tired. I am tired. Could be from the weekend still, could be the non-stop nursing. Baby Girl is on the floor and I should be putting out the trash in this time.

Busy weekend, too much time out. Too much too much too much. Red Sox win tonight and it feels late because the game is over. Last week games at Gerrit's, games and debates and what's the difference? Hitchhikers turn into white crosses. Memorial mass and Abby could be a Catholic for Halloween, no?

Turn the heat on, steam out the back of the furnace. Basement full of steam, no heat, new valves no use and the oil man on the way. Two trips later and heat for the baby, quiet hissing in each room. This will be the soundtrack to our lives.

I don't know what to do tomorrow. Aside from the list of things I have been putting off. Insurance company, IRS, thank-you notes and scones. I should build radiator covers before the baby can crawl. Abigail is watching the debate. All she sees is contrast.

TUESDAY, OCTOBER 5

INSTEAD OF FALLING back asleep after Baby Girl nursed this morning I am up and running. Trash out, two hand-me-down air conditioners moved from upstairs to down, kitty litter cleaned. Coffee half decaf today. If I am going to drink it all day I must compromise.

Fourteen of my father's old shirts are in the middle of my living room floor. My brother is having a baby. Naming him after my father. The shower is Saturday and I am making a quilt. From these shirts. From Richard. For Richard.

I never called my father Richard. Most called him Rick. I heard someone call him Dick in the supermarket once and decided then that I didn't like the name. It didn't worry me since I never used it. But after he died and I didn't know which kind the baby in my belly was I felt guilty, like maybe I should think of it. Like it is the right thing to do.

Funny that last day he was conscious, just barely. Monthly check-up in the morning, happy to be just about over the miscarriage-hump, twelve weeks and hurrah! Celebratory sandwich at The Grange, mostly to see Zac, and when I finally got home twelve messages on the machine. He's not doing well. They're rushing him home in an ambulance to die. They don't think he'll make it that long. Meet at the house. Go to Mass General.

He wasn't talking anymore when we got there but was smiling and squeezing hands and when I told him the baby was fine, heard a heartbeat, this one is going to make it he squeezed my hand and smiled. Tear in his eye. He was so happy I was pregnant.

Now my baby is asleep across the room. The silly aqua and white shirt with the knit collar is on top of the pile. I am making a quilt for Richard out of it and for the life of me I can't do it. The Porter line will continue. What the hell does that mean? Last names. City officials shake my brother's hand, recognize him by name. And they will do the same for his baby. Pay reverence to the name. As Abigail sleeps in near anonymity.

I've got to take scissors to the shirts on the floor. Cut them up. Make something new. I wish I had religion right now, that I believed he is somewhere looking down on what I am doing. That he sees Abigail in her cradle. That he's seen her smile. She's cooing now, in her sleep. I've got to go.

THURSDAY, OCTOBER 14

TRUTH BE TOLD I am sick of cool. Like heavy talk with an upspeak like having a dream of talking like talking like yeah. Black and white and drunk and my art and yeah and wow. Of winning and losing and co-authors and blocking projects knit by other people. Complaining and matter and driving around looking at signs— Welcome home sailors and marines and soldiers and No More Bush and Lordy Lordy.

I have to admit I don't understand my boiler. How to keep the water in the glass tube right and which way to turn the vents. Can't afford to have the guy come show me and don't have the guts to admit it anyway. May go to the heating supply store near the state fish pier and ask with babe on my hip. It's cheaper that way. I need a new vent anyway.

What is this crap movie? Animated people talking about dreams. Crap. Referring to Lorca, of course.

I am also sick of weird.

If there are beautiful women at a party and I don't feel beautiful I am not one of them. I do not feel beautiful. I feel more like a machine. There is a list of things that need to be done and I will turn myself on and do them. I will turn myself off and rest. Repeat. No, that's not true. I wish I felt like a machine. There is a list of things I need to do but because I feel about too many things I can't seem to get them done.

I wish I were watching Monday Night Football with Jim Dunn.

Bills keep coming bills are always coming and no one no one knows how to pay them. Camper has a monkey shoe I can't resist but will. Tomorrow might bring me to Portsmouth for Kerry but the baby's in charge and I have no definite plans. Monkey shoes are in Portsmouth. Monkey shoes or boiler? Heat or food or fashion?

I need to say this before I forget: Fuck Curt Schilling.

MONDAY, NOVEMBER 1

OIL BURNER'S BROKE again, we all have to break sometime. Ice cream is cheaper than Zoloft and doing the dishes tonight makes tomorrow better. Even if it's cold. Abby's talking to a ball and I am trying to keep a positive solitaire score until the diapers are ready for the drier. Or is it dryer? For the life of me I can't remember. Abby's talking is nearing crying.

Spit up on my shoulder and I wonder what will give next. The neighbor tried to trade the cover of my garbage can for his ratty one in the wind this morning. Caught in the act. Not that he thought mine was his but it was easier than looking.

Electric heat upstairs so we won't be so cold. Isn't there always something to complain about? Life is good here with this little girl, her coos and smiles, and still I throw disinfecting wipes across the room. Because I don't get upset often I shouldn't get upset and when I do it doesn't show so tonight I throw things and they come to an abrupt stop under the cold radiator. A couple tears and that doesn't help anything, family is still family and ashes thrown to Ipswich Bay can not be gotten back. Decisions made can not be changed when pride is on the line. You can't make a son visit his mother or a father visit his daughter. You can't stop a train wreck even if you see it happening.

Coffee with Gerrit this afternoon. Got a package from Glasgow, registered mail, signed for it at the post office. Walked down Dale Ave next to a man in Patriots gear who talked to me the whole time. Saw a woman at the Lone Gull who sort of knew me but couldn't figure how.

Spoke with Jack at Mystery Train about babies and writing.

Abigail keeps turning her head like it's all the rage. Talk to the curtain. Wave at the light. Peek-a-boo! I see you.

I wish there were more Moomin books to read. That someone would stop by and say "Hey, want to go get a quick drink?" That politicians didn't interrupt soap operas. That I got more mail.

Why is it so hard to call repair people? Other people don't think they should be plumbers, carpenters and electricians. Why does it make me feel so useless?

WEDNESDAY, NOVEMBER 3

THE THING ABOUT it is that you never know when someone is thinking about you. My ficus tree is dropping its leaves, I haven't found a place it likes in this house yet. Ficus generation.

I don't know what my options are but for this: I must not add to the confusion. Two new valves for radiators. I will master this system by spring. I need a mirror and clear plastic. Power tools and foam.

I used to read things and hope that they were written for me. I know better now.

BATHTUB CAULKED, CEILING painted.
Everything done means something left undone.

FIRST TAKE OUT the rocks and the jackets then take the car to Linsky's. No coffee left in the house so stop at Uncle Moe's. Jack says: Hello Beautiful. Jack says: I know you love coffee. Grilled cheese, turkey soup, coffee. Old woman comes in. Plumber comes in and tells her she has a flat tire. Guys at the counter banter, argue about who can and who will help her out. Banter ends with no resolution until I offer to change her tire. Someone gets up to do it right away.

Home now to balance the checkbook. See how much, for when the mechanic calls. Sounds like the head gasket. How much is too much? How long is too long? She's a good car, I'd hate to see her go.

JAMES IS SNIFFLING, time for soup. Into the truck, to the market, to play our favorite game. Best Shopper. Come home with everything we need while saving the most money. Today I win with thirty four percent.

Onions, garlic, carrots, celery in the pot. Chicken and water. Boil. And boil. And boil. Remove chicken, strain. Add new onions and garlic cut smaller than needed. Add carrots and celery. Add broth. Pick chicken.

When picking a chicken be sure to have a bowl of cold water handy for when you burn your fingers. My first chicken picked in this house. Counters are different so I set myself up new. Put the old vegetables in a second pot and add whatever parts of the chicken are not going in the soup. Add water and boil for a second batch of broth to freeze.

Careful with the chicken. Growing up a knuckle or two found their way into my soup. Unpleasant to find. Some people like it, like they like tendon or tripe. My grandmother would gnaw at the ends of chicken wings.

Add chipotle peppers, roasted corn. Simmer. Make a grilled cheese with red onion, Dijon mustard and tomato. Test soup. Try not to turn the television on. Sunday night, baby nursing and I'm not tired enough to go to sleep. I will regret this in the morning.

MONDAY, DECEMBER 6

2005

ONE YEAR AGO cold air phone call quick ride crying to the city to MGH. Time for a few words him listening me talking baby's good, going to be okay, love you. Love you. Tried to get up can't get up can't talk smiles and tear in his eye. Morphine drip drip swab his mouth keep him comfortable hold his hand. To the chapel comfort sister to the gift shop busy the boys to the  cafeteria salad bar and the hallway coffee shop. Gift shop stationery green with white edges and pad with dots and pen. Write letters never sent. Gift store again sample sale baby clothes for the wee one to be. Brother gives blood borrow shirt sleep in scrubs solitaire knit and read. Ice from the nurse's station drinks from vending machines backpack brought in with things we need. Pizza boxes on the window sill brother on the floor father not opening his eyes second night no response heart slowing third day waiting watching holding hand ball to squeeze swab his mouth keep him comfy talk and talk new nurses familiar from before transplant doctors come to say goodbye pay respects. Take the elevator to the top floors Blake 10 nice waiting room look over the Charles he was here once come up at night stars and dark and feel alone alone alone but sister's there and we are alone. Tired worn out getting toward peaceful time for bed Sam and me in one him in the other stepmother next to him go to sleep we're all going to sleep together family-like and we sleep two three hours nurses come in Jane wakes us he's gone. Wake up relieved hug each other kiss his forehead hold his hand hand on head again goodbye and put my head on the bed and cry. Say thank you, thank you gather our stuff pack it up clean up pizza boxes call people say goodbye elevator down hospital empty walk outside into the cold first time in days cold air cold drive home route one drive east into the sunrise.

Miss you, Da, love you.

TALKING TODAY ABOUT family and lovers. A lesson in how to fall in love. A lesson in how to be in love.

I had a dream the other night, I'll tell you about it later. Ran into a friend. Not in the dream. Thought of you, all of you.

I can't even remember who my friends are anymore.

Give the baby three oranges and watch her roll them around. Take a walk in the cold. Remember that you have a body. Remember what that means.

Sometimes these things come back to me: a smile, a hand, the way the phone rings. I am trying to make these things into rag dolls. Not like poets do but with fabric and yarn. Most of it scraps.

I wish you would call or write. I have more to say about lovers and more to say about family.

THURSDAY, JANUARY 13

SITTING AT A show outside snow is getting dirty and dirtier until it is only dirt.

Some things look like butterflies and some things look like butterflies with no middles.

Sad to think that nobody knows your mind and sad to know that nobody's trying but it doesn't mean you are unloved just that you are alone.

Funny how each of us has a body.

Funny how somebody can step out of your life for some time and expect there to be a place holder.

Like we don't all work in waves.

F LICKING BASEBALL CARDS at the wall, my room best in the corner near the door. Sort cards by brand by team by position. Different cards for different purposes but for flicking only one good luck: Mookie Wilson.

THERE'S ALWAYS TOO much of something and tonight I'm afraid it's me. Winter won't end and I don't know what I'd do if it did. Spring is rebirth full of new and I can't let go of the old. Old and dead ideas. Old and dead hellos. Old and dead goodbyes.

The tide is turning. The tide is always turning. Trust me, boys. What's low now will be high again.

WEDNESDAY, MARCH 9

I DON'T HAVE a dog and I don't smoke but my yard is filled with cigarette butts and dog shit. Snow melted, leaving the yard covered in sand and shit and somebody's broken trash can. Wednesday, at least, trash day, fill the broken barrel and set it out.

I've been finding new uses for baby food jars. Good for trapping pale spiders. Good as shot glasses. Good for keeping things one shouldn't keep. Half the jars get cleaned, thrown in the drawer near the cat food. Half the jars end up in the recycling. One jar is open on the table on the deck, spider web down the center.

Being an expert starter I am trying to become a better finisher. My daily lists have turned to catalogs of projects I have started already. Finish blue sweater. Put laundry away. Finish paying bills. Clean up from previous projects. Yarn toys sand dishes clothing papers books music.

I have letters to write.

WEDNESDAY, MARCH 30

MONDAY MORNING IN bed reading trying to wait for baby's morning smiles. Lists are forming (lists are always forming) things to do: Get up! Obligations. What comes first? Try to manage priorities. Taxes, of course. Which means to the library. To the library—a walk! A walk. Of course.

To the library. I need to find my library card first.

To do:
Find library card.
Walk to library.

Look for a book on retaining walls and building raised beds. For my garden. My yard. Yes, my yard. There is one, there, even if it is small and touching other properties. Some of us need to live right up close. Find a book on living up close and still growing things.

To do:
Grows things.

Two Concord grape vines in a box in the cellar. The back yard (the neighbor's front) gets sun and the property line allows for an inch or two of it. Vines could grow up to the deck. They'll need a little protection from the kids and the dog.

To do:
Buy some fence.

Buy some fence, little fence. Maybe that silly scalloped wire stuff. A little something to put around the base. And maybe some soil, and maybe some railroad ties. And bricks. Bricks for a walkway and maybe a stair. I need a book on laying brick walks. And sand for under the bricks.

Mrs. Ramsey is knitting. One project finished last night, need to send it off. Sew a tag inside. Directions for another found, it nearly finished. And the back of the baby sweater from my second pregnancy. Can't bear to finish it for another child, can't take it out. I could turn it into pillow. I should finish living projects first.

To do:
Sew tag.
Knit.
Go to the post office.

Reading still, list getting longer. Abigail whimpers. Put the book down and give her my breast. Lily and her oils. I wonder what my mother's work would look like in oil. If I could paint in oil. Can I get oil paints on my walk? In my dream a few weeks back the art store only opened two days a week and sold political scarves. I am sure they have oil paints as well. Maybe Jane would paint with me. On the deck. Maybe I should paint the deck. No, it will do as it is. But the front porch needs painting.

To do:
Buy oil paints.
Call Jane.
Strip porch.
Paint.

All these lists and still in bed. Abby's asleep. I should get something done. Want to stay with her, stay in bed to get the first morning smiles. I can sneak away, put away the last of the maternity clothes, start a load of laundry, do last night's dishes.

To do:
Get up.
Put clothes away.
Do dishes.
Start laundry.

Up now, monitor on, Abby upstairs and she starts to coo. To tht-tht-tht and daa-daa-daa.

To do:
Miss morning smiles.

S PRING IN FULL bloom in Seattle hints of honeysuckle in the air. Abigail pulling her socks off to celebrate the weather. She takes over the job of flirting: record-store boys and restaurateurs fall at her feet.

THURSDAY, MAY 12

TODAY IS MY father's birthday and I want it to be noted there are cedar timbers in my yard yes my yard and I ate a processed meat sandwich this evening and tried hard to enjoy sitting. My peas are several inches tall. I didn't go to the cemetery. My grandfather won't go to the zoo.

Today I did the work I had to do. Today is my father's birthday. Tomorrow is Monday tomorrow I clean the house and today I leave dishes in the sink. I knit until my fingers hurt. Today I don't call people I should and I don't call people who think I should. Today I woke up tired.

Tomorrow I will clean the dog shit out of the yard. I will put the folded laundry away. I will vacuum the floor and pay the bills. Tonight I will go upstairs to the people I love. Today is my father's birthday. I want it to be noted.

SUN-BURNT SKIN IN a deep v, cheeks and nose and chin. Woke with a start to a dream of morning, this morning, and all the done things still needing to be done. One hundred and twenty finger sandwiches. Iced tea. Lemonade.

Trying to catch up all week to slow down and catch up clean up and slow down. Hoping for that time when the things that hang are done and the ideas that pass are noted. Eleven squares of thrift-store fabric, varying sizes, still quite separate and slightly undone.

Clean the study, put the gate up. Think of notes to write. Notes to write. Try to keep the dishes clean, try to avoid ants. Wash diapers. Wash clothes. Try to think of what to say. Try to think of how to put eleven squares together.

Paper plates. Paper cups. Knife for the watermelon. Tablecloth. Trying to remember how to hide what I am thinking. Trying to figure out when I lost that skill. Buy a cake: Glosta Rocks. Bowls for chips. Four bags of ice. Kiddy pool.

Fiesta gone, Viva! Viva! Me on the beach alone in a crowd eating a sausage from Ambie. Funny to think that anybody looking at me can see what I am thinking. Watch the greasy pole, watch the crowd. Try to make note of fashion.

Is it having a baby? Never being alone? There are a good number of things in anybody's head that don't need to come out. Moments of sadness. Distraction. Frustration. Things that are no less real if they are private. Things that are no more real if they show.

Abby miserable in the heat, heat rash and sweat. Can't sleep. Won't eat. Better after the rain, waking happy and kissing me again. She is learning from me how to be. Kissing and smiling and cooing in the back of her throat.

I am trying to be alone more often. Trying to have my feelings alone. Alone being with Abigail, of course. It hasn't done anybody any good to know what I am thinking. There are so many parts to life, so much to feel about. I am red like a lobster and my skin hurts. I have talked about hats with important people and they may know I don't care. That can't be nice for them.

DRIVE IN TO the meeting, game on. New place. Hard to park. Small turnout, the usual suspects, carded at the bar and a Guinness for me.

No point to the meeting. No point. The boys and I sitting around. Me trying not to mind the drive in for nothing. The boys talking about nothing. Mike Wallace. Renter's market.

Turn to nostalgia: children's shows, coal fires. Matt wanting to go back in time. Seven kids, two parents, coal fire and fresh fruit scones. Better then. So I try and I can't think of a time I would want to go back to. Can't think of a time that is better than this.

Wait at the bar, game over. I don't know Brighton. One-way streets, no choices, cop behind me. Just keep going. I don't know the streets. Don't know Brighton. Keep going. Drive until things look familiar, kind of, tracks down the road and finally a sign. Beacon Street through Brookline past Coolidge Corner. Beacon Street into the heart of the monster.

Asshole fans in their SUVs and I am too tired. Trying to think of a time. Wood stove, three kids curled up in front. Mom with her hand through the glass door. Robert crying every day, running away just out of sight. Asshole fans cutting me off and blocking the roads and honking.

Try a side street to get away. It is blocked by fans clogging intersections.

Turn around. Run away. Back up Beacon to North Harvard. Middle school. Drinking and lying and trying to get away, friends' parents dying of heroin overdoses and men grabbing my breasts. Jane yelling at my mother and making me diet. Dad getting sick and us starting to know it.

Down North Harvard, into Allston. Familiar places all the way. Road work on the bridge, Storrow Drive instead. High School. Galen dying. Willie killing himself. Stephen dying. Always thinking someone would die and not really being far off. Restraining order and running away and looking out at the ocean crying. Staying up at friends' houses after everyone was asleep and looking out the window. Crying. Trying to make it.

Storrow Drive down to one lane and the assholes join in. So tired my eyes are drooping when it dawns on me: I have never been happier than I am now. I love my husband. I love my baby. I don't think anyone I love is dying. I am responsible for myself. I like my life.

Me in every period before this exploding with joy. Beaming. Me trying so hard to be happy. And now I wake up and Abigail kisses me. I don't have to do a thing. I don't have to try.

Route 1 and I am tired and hungry and thinking of course about what must be wrong. Something must always be wrong. And the saddest thing I realize is people dying unhappy. Not just sad but so far gone there is no joy. My mother. I want her to be happy. I don't want anything else for her or from her. Just to be happy. She used to beam and laugh and be happy but it's been months since I heard her cackle. And then the other saddest thing. The people I love hurt each other.

Nearly crying now thinking of how much someone I love has hurt people. I need to stop. I need to get something to keep me awake and keep me going. Mind's on grand mal seizures and hospital rooms and stories not believed and whole histories being dismissed.

Drive-Thru. 24 hours. Pull over, search for change. Get to the menu and I just want something to drink but late night, limited menu. The woman doesn't understand me and I don't understand her and because I can't figure out how to get just a drink I end up with a meal.

Back on the road caffeine and fries and I really have been happy for most of my life. But I don't want to go back. Local boy, grown man now, arrested last week trying to get back to before his brother died, spray-painting mailboxes to remember. I don't want to go back. Past the mall's empty lots flashing lights on the south-bound side. I was happy then. I did happy things.

Awake now, mind racing, burger uneaten. Home to sports radio left on downstairs. Hoping someone is awake for me to see for me to say I love you. I am happy. But they are upstairs asleep and my mind is racing. Each of these things so full so good and bad like swabbing my father's mouth as he died. There is comfort in everything.

These are the things I did. These are the things I remember. Tomorrow is trash day and I don't want to bring it all out tonight. I should go to sleep if I want to get it done before the truck comes tomorrow. When I was in young I would sit on the rock barely peeping through the part of our yard near the street and wait for the trashmen to come. I still love the sound of their trucks.

T ODAY IS A day for doing things. Today is a day for getting things done. Today the toys go where they belong, with the toys they belong with. One room of the dollhouse for chairs and tables. One for musical instruments. One for blocks. One for puzzles.

Today is a day for eating well. Broccoli for the baby and rice for us both. No meat on the grill today. Too much rain. Too much meat. No cake for the baby. Not too much coffee for me.

Today is a day to do little things. Nail the carpet back onto the last step. Cut back plants and start new ones. Mark hand-me-downs for ownership.

Today is a day to ignore the past. Boxes of memories left alone. People not called. Stories not thought of. Letters not answered. Feelings denied.

Today is a day for today. Baby at the piano banging notes. Composter built on the living room floor. Cake for me. Ask Jane about birthdays. Colors on baby and paper and chair. Music instead of news. Bare feet and jeans.

GARDEN THINNED, LEAVES falling on the back deck. Wool finally feeling good in my hands, needles clicking quicker. Baby walking half-way across rooms, kicking balls and kissing dolls. Bath in the pool outside, wind whispers and neighbors chatter, bubbly hair and foam alphabet.

Soup weather. Soup season, at least. Cut the leeks under running water, clean the dirt between the layers. Baby walking and falling and crying. Too tired to be awake but not sleepy. Melt butter in a pot. Add leeks. Put Abigail upstairs and listen to her sing to herself. Sing to the cat. The window. The clothes she pulls off her father's dresser and into the crib. Coos and quiet and coos.

Today is Wednesday. What does that mean? It doesn't mean anything anymore. Water the plants with water from the rain barrel. Add the bowl of vegetable ends to the compost pile. Pay the bills. At least most of them. Wash the diapers, hang them in the sun. Wash the tub. Knit a sweater for the naked doll.

Abigail is quiet now, quiet for some time. The leeks smell like they may be ready for broth and potatoes. My sewing room is clean now, piles for each project: the shirt quilt for Greg and Kari, the chicken quilt I have to start. Finished knitting projects. Knitting projects that just need finishing. Knitting projects just barely started. Notions. Notions! Abigail is cooing again.

So many tomatoes I am thinking of canning.

WEDNESDAY, SEPTEMBER 14   122

U P EARLY, DOWNSTAIRS, soup's out again still cold. Me dressed. Abby dressed. Forget shoes and sweaters and keys. Gather quarters and leave.

Walk downtown past the smells. Smells of caramel and bread and coffee and donuts. Past churches and chairs on the sidewalk and large appliances out for pickup. To the cafe. Espresso for me, sesame cookie for Abby. Sicilian talk of soccer and Sox.

Out of money. Go home or get more? To the bank then to Two Sisters. Too many dishes at home and the instant decision not to wash them yet, not just yet. Call Gerrit. Breakfast for me and Abby, Gerrit and Greg talking art and crotches. Twice as much as breakfast in the Fort.

Walk home, sometimes raining, just a drop here and there. Spitting, really. Telling Abigail the names of flowers. This is a morning glory, this is a rose. Maybe we'll eat every meal out today and I won't do any dishes. This is hibiscus. Tired of measuring my value in cleanliness. Look at the sunflowers.

Graves of sea captains with ships on them. Ben Pine, Columbia. Ordered yarn last night, super-bulky alpaca. Colors like the sunrise. Seashell pink and thistle down and starlight blue. I may not clean at all today. The sky is opening and I've had too much coffee. That won't keep me from drinking more. Abigail making wookie noises and watching break dancing on television. Something's got to give.

THURSDAY, SEPTEMBER 15

I AM SITTING.

I am sitting down.

I am sitting down in a room filled with paper and books and puzzles and bags. Two pound-a-balls and a husband and a cat. Three pairs of scissors and six rolls of tape and a tree that needs watering. I am sitting down and I am not getting up.

2006

DREAMING A LOT lately, dreaming at night. Snakes in the gutters feet long and green. Nick Drake in an antique and yarn store at the mall, working and happy that people think he's dead. Living below my grandfather or above my grandfather and stuck there, stuck there. A deck all around the house and a dog rushing toward us, toward Abigail. Woods like where we used to play near Tide Rock.

Green. Green everywhere.

I DON'T EVEN know what to say about today.

Lottery. Purple scrunchie. Brother's Deli. Black and blue. Still lost.

S AND EVERYWHERE. ERRANDS run, baby asleep unexpectedly and nothing to do about it but drive. Eighteen-wheeler blocking rotary traffic. Policemen and DPW blocking Washington.

Sand everywhere.

Men in expensive cars try to cut me off. Gesture when I don't yield. I don't yield. I won't yield.

Seven messages on the answering machine. Amanda? Amanda? I don't know what to do. Hang up. Amanda? Hello? Seven messages in ten minutes. I am not going home.

All morning spent paying bills. Opening mail. Budgeting and planning. All morning. Peanut butter on my shirt, out of two-cent stamps, tired in my head. Sand everywhere and I'm not going home. Men in expensive cars trying to cut me off but I keep driving.

FRIDAY, MARCH 3

THEY SAY AS she grew older she shrank into a shadow of the people around her.

YESTERDAY CLOUDS CROUCHED over the city like tigers ready to pounce. Today the air is warmer and the sky is blue. This morning with a bad start, sick stomach and tired eyes, overheard conversations and a tumble down the front steps.

Trying to fill the day with knitting and cleaning. Trying to make that enough. Sweaters drying on the deck, dishes waiting in the sink. Sit on sandy steps. Watch trucks take trash.

Hope for a better afternoon. Hope it is better before noon. Hope for better.

WEDNESDAY, MARCH 8

S HE DOESN'T LIKE the picture of herself.

She was in an argument. Someone was yelling at her. She decided to drive away.

In Hamilton she came across a work horse. A big horse, tan, with black hair. Its tail was thirty feet long. It reared, its hooves right next to her. Its back was dappled. It jumped over her. It was just inches away.

It is probably still there.

What is the name of the baby she gets pictures of? She asked that of them, that they name him that. She asked that they name him Richard.

At the art store she has two canvases, fifteen inches by thirty inches. She needs to pay for a tube of white paint she took another day. She has some canvas she needs to have stretched. Not here, the canvas is at home.

She has a wallet full of quarters. She takes out her bills and leaves them on the counter. She takes the quarters out and hands them to the man. Four, five dollars. Another handful. Seven, eight dollars. One more. Thirteen dollars in quarters. Sixteen dollars in bills.

He'll wait until next time, he says. I pay for the rest. It's easier to remember that way.

At the hardware store she says she wants to spend a thousand dollars today. She tells the story of the man who is always convulsing. The story of the war over trash can covers. She shows me a rock in the shape of a bird. A rock that is a heart.

We drink iced coffee. She offers me her cookbooks. We drive around the coast. Ah, aquamarine. She tells the story of the sixteen-foot seal she found on the rocks. Dead. She didn't smell it because the wind was the other way. Its nails were so long.

At home she has a picture of their baby hanging next to the picture of a baby from a frame. The frame dimensions written on his chest. She has a new painting. A tree of life. A new tree of life.

I BOUGHT ROSES with Gerrit on Monday. He makes me buy flowers. He makes faces at Abigail. He coos and beeps. He says people think he is her grandfather. He beeps. I am missing a father. He coos.

They put vaseline in her hair. They make her sit. They make her drink a horrible drink. She can't find his phone number.

I am cold. I have avocado to eat and dill havarti. Abigail is singing upstairs, sailing to Botany Bay. I am missing a grandfather. I don't want to do anything. I have bills to pay.

We watch the trash truck come. Our barrel is only half full. I don't believe them when they say this is spring.

The heat comes on. For the first time in years she is at appointments without me. They put vaseline in her hair without even asking. It won't come out for days. They make her sit still. Tomorrow I won't be there when they tell her what it means. I'll be getting pictures of the baby in my belly. I can't tell her they didn't hurt her. Can't help her remember my name. I can't tell them when she counts her children four. Can't tell them when I do the same.

YOU CAN SEE the smoke from Stage Fort Park. Clouds of smoke from behind the hospital. He died in Florida, his first vacation in twelve years. It is hard to tell at first where the smoke is from. Lanesville? Annisquam? He had come from seeing the Red Sox in spring training. Driving down the Boulevard and up Centennial the smoke looks like the other clouds. Hit by a car. Frank from Gloucester isn't calling any shows for a week to show his respect.

The rotary is too low, can't see the smoke. Passing Addison Gilbert I see it. Up to Wheeler's Point. They brought the World Series trophy to see him at the restaurant. Uncle Moe's. Down the streets to the left there smoke between the houses but no fire. No engines. Tommy Moses, local softball legend. Turn around, up Cocaine Lane. The smoke is closer to the water. Down Cherry Street. Toward the rotary. Up over the bridge. At the restaurant he called me beautiful, got me coffee. He knew how much I liked coffee. Turn around at exit twelve. Him noting Abigail getting bigger. Back up over the bridge.

There is fire, open flames on Pole's Hill.

O PENING DAY. 1:25, Abby down for a nap. All day preparing. Buy seeds, pansies, gloves and a trowel. Borrow wagon. Buy potting soil, composted manure.

Find extension cord. Radio outside. Batteries for the monitor. Glass of water.

Last year's tomatoes, vines pale and dead, pull them out. Sweep sand from the top of the soil. Litter and leaves. Bamboo stakes.

Add peat moss. Add manure. Turn over, turn under. Gather seeds. Sugar Snap and Dwarf Gray Sugar peas. Bloomsdale spinach. Mesclun and mustard greens. Early Wonder beet and Cherry Belle radish. Bunching onion and Danvers Half Long carrot.

Bending over. Heartburn. Mark rows with broken stakes. Peas down the middle. Red Sox up by two. Sun gone, skin cold. Plant pansies on the stairs. Big Papi. Inside, dirty clothes off, jammies on. There's a lot to like about Lowell. Knit in bed next to a sleeping baby. Thank goodness for Coco Crisp.

MONDAY, APRIL 3

I WISH THINGS were as lovely as cherry blossoms fallen on grass.

TUESDAY, APRIL 18

TRASH OUT FROM the back when the white truck moves. Recycling out but not the paper. Not the cardboard. Toilet broken and fixed.

Baby crying in gasps on the telephone. Cat walking on the keyboard. Laundry on the floor and dishes in the sink. Stomach upset from chemical drinks and leftover ham.

Husband away. Peas coming up. Llama in the living room and pansies in the car. Letters photocopied. Baseball game on.

List of things to do. Seeds to plant. Curtains to fix. Rooms to clean and checkbooks to balance. Lonely, lonesome or alone?

WAKE UP THIRTY. Cuddle in bed with the baby girl, tickle tickle wee.

Decide to take the day slowly. Sister calls, coffee then off to renew my license. No line no hassle. Something at the yarn store but not too much. Wool and cotton for the baby in my belly. Sister's again, a box of color, and home with the decision to do what I want. Email from Amanda and note from Zac. Father-in-law and brother-in-law. Flowers and Hamlet Machine when James gets home. Abby to Tad and Jane's, us off to sushi. Coffee.

Back to pick up Abby. Knit sushi from Jane! Home now, baby in bed, James asleep. Two messages. Birthday wishes from my brother. Stepmother calling to see if we will see her on Mother's Day.

Chuckle to myself, chuckle here. Happy to be thirty, happy to be me. Happy I can giggle thinking of who remembers and who doesn't. Happy to know what matters.

FEELING LIKE AN orphan. Tired, worn out, coffee in bed, slow waking. Trying hard not to avoid things. People. Phone calls.

Mother quiet today, not hearing and not talking. The same questions again and again. I'm tired and I don't know what to do. We drive, around and around. She isn't hungry. She's starving. Just a soda. Coffee. Salad would be good. I default and spend more than I should on lunch to have an easy place, a place she knows. For the third time this year this is the first time we've gone.

Dropping her off she is tired and thankful. No words but thank you, thank you for coming. Abby says her name. I say her name. Across the street the near-blind and the drunk are waiting to catch the bus.

MONDAY, JUNE 5

HEAT EVERYWHERE. CARS drive by with radios blaring. Kids light fireworks in the park. It is summer no matter how I try to deny it.

These are things I have meant to say:

The perfect tree on my street blossomed and then lost all of its blossoms. The little girl in the back yard has been stealing my peas. I saw the guy who looks like Jim at the market again. Small strokes.

The drive to Lynn was less rewarding than I had hoped.

Strawberries and rhubarb, heavy cream. Peas with ginger and garlic. Morning sickness all over again. Tired, tired, tired. Belly big and ankles swollen. Counting down in weeks.

Baby sleeping. She's not so baby anymore, with letters and please and nipple and coffee. Trying to make this last month of just her count. Cuddle, read, kiss and tickle.

World Cup fever.

THANK GOODNESS THERE'S a cop at Tony's Porn and Lotto Mart. Me with my pram and the guy in the wheelchair playing Keno, barely enough room for one of us nevermind two vehicles. Talking with the guy who collects scrap metal about those immigrants. They're workaholics. Take $10 an hour even if the going rate is $23. And the Americans are so lazy—they win a few bucks on a scratch ticket, go out and get drunk, don't show up the next day. The cop directs me to the ramp, exit 12, he says, Seabrook, New Hampshire. Crosses his fingers in prayer for Samuel's health. Calls me good girl for my Moxie.

COMING HOME FROM the orchard, a car burnt out just south of exit 15. Vermont plates, fire engine, ambulance, police cars. Trees turning red around us. Coming up on October. It'll be here soon, then November and December. Months get cold and colder.

On the second floor in the T.V. room we sat and ate oranges before bed. Marnie would peel them and split them between us. Elizabeth in her red and white pajamas. Robert in his velour tiger suit. A hug and a bug and a love and a kiss before bed. Us in the big house with our grandparents, her home alone in an empty room that would be mine. Crying.

When she was little she would climb into the bread oven beside the fireplace in the tv room and close the door. As he was emptying the house she climbed in again, in with old postcards and lost scrabble letters, the snakeskin from Peter's move west. The room almost empty but for the pictures on the mantle and my grandfather's grandfather's cradle. Pictures cut out and glued to a board, kids in turtlenecks. Judy smiling.

T O THINK ABOUT it wakes me up at night.

When Judy got sick they flew her east. They gave her the bedroom we had slept in and the tv room on the second floor. They scoffed at her diet of whole grains and raw vegetables.

When she got sicker they wheeled her out into the sun on a new wrought-iron chaise lounge. She sat in the sun and tanned. She sat in the sun and grew new hair as her baby girl walked on the grass of the hill. She sat in the sun while her eyes got empty. After I saw her for the last time I watched the parade from the corner in front of the art store. Two days later she was dead.

I know a man who kept his toenail clippings in a decorated pill box next to the bed. He slept under a print of two men sleeping next to each other. His lover's daughter thought it was a picture of her father twice.

QUIET NIGHT, READING in bed when it comes in through the window like an anthem—the theme song for M*A*S*H. Almost every day for five years after Marnie got sick it came up the stairwell to our place. Almost every night growing up it came through the wall from my mother's room. For at least half of my life, one of the steadiest things I knew.

This morning cleaning like the Queen is coming. Sam nursing and crying and sleeping, nursing and sleeping and crying. Abby walking around with her doll singing a song to herself: Don't cry, Mommy, don't cry. Kitchen and bathroom mopped, chairs scrubbed, counters clean. Soup on the stove, soup on the stove. By six o'clock the three of us are sitting in the middle of a pile of laundry to fold, one of us crying. By nine I am the only one awake and not much of the day's work shows. By ten-thirty the kitchen is clean again and I am done.

WEDNESDAY, SEPTEMBER 20

S HE IS LYING on the table in a fetal position facing the wall. She looks younger this way, her skin smooth and her fancy underwear with a bow on the back. I stand at her head with my hand on the side of her face.

He feels her back, finds her spine. An inch out of place and nobody ever notices. Presses firmly here, and there, looking for the right place. He paints her back with an antiseptic sponge. Frames her spine with paper.

A shot to mask the pain. She doesn't flinch, she is sedated. The next needle shudders as it hits bone, stops and starts as it looks for a way through. I rub her cheek as she moans. It hurts, it hurts. Out and in again. Prodding.

He stops and looks for something else to stop the pain. I help him get the bottle out of the cabinet, hold it at an angle so he can fill the syringe. I wash my hands afterward thinking I should have washed them first. I hold her head as he pricks her again.

The baby starts crying. We trade places, Ralph and I. The needle goes in again. She cries. The baby cries. Pain down her leg, her hip, her knees. I start to nurse. Blood trickles down her back. Ralph holds her head as she cries out, whimpers, moans. Her ankles hurt. Her left leg jerks. She cries out in pain.

The baby is quiet. The needle moves in and out. Ralph is holding her head. She is crying. Nearly the right spot. Her legs kick. Ralph is holding her head. He tells her to be strong. Be strong for the babies. She is crying. Blood is trickling down her back.

Ten minutes. Twenty minutes. Thirty minutes. Nearly an hour gone and finally it comes down the needle: clear fluid, like water dripping from a leaf. She is quiet as we watch it fall, drip by drip, into the vial. One vial. He turns the needle to see if it will flow faster. Two vials. She mutters and her body starts to unfold. Three vials. Four vials full from the needle in her spine. He takes out the needle. She is still as he washes her back. Puts a bandaid on.

I want to remember this so I don't judge her too harshly.

SUNDAY, NOVEMBER 19

I DIDN'T TELL you about the dream I had a few weeks back. Pinochet's brain became part of my head at the back, and a mob was leading me around the city looking for the right place to execute Pinochet. When they had me up at Willowrest I saw my sister in the crowd. I could feel his brain mixing with mine at the edges and I wanted to see him dead. All I could do was let the crowd lead me.

Candies, fruit and Jewish foods are on sale. I buy chips for the party. Cream to make more egg nog. At the checkout I see a can I thought was artichokes is chick peas. The girl double-bags glass bottles of pear juice. The boy puts them in more bags before putting them in my cart.

Driving home it is still snowing. This is what it will be like for her—white covering things she knows are there, covering them until she questions what is there, until she forgets what was there altogether and then that anything was there at all.

At home Sam is coughing like a seal. Abigail is walking in circles looking for chocolate, saying I am so lucky. I am so lucky.

2007

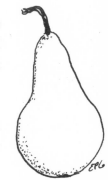

T RYING TO FIGURE what it means to be remembered, why it matters. A cold morning. I remember that. A boarding pass to Shannon. A present never mailed.

Cleaning my desk, finding things I may have forgotten. A string of beads. An old violin. Letters written and not mailed. Letters received and not returned.

Trying to think of why it matters to be remembered. Graveyards full, full of people. Graveyards full of people I know. People I knew. People I remember. Graveyards full of forgotten people.

Smiles of a summer night. My grandmother, feet on the coffee table, drinking coffee out of a small white mug and watching old movies. I remember the swans swimming, candles growing long tails. What of this remembering? Red velveteen. Smoking on walks around the block, then only in the bathroom, then not at all. Cherries soaked in her Manhattans. Eating oranges before bed.

I tried this morning to remember my father's voice. How he answered the phone. Gave advice. I'm not sure I got it but I remembered the way he looked when there was nothing he could do. I remember his look. Sympathy. Empathy.

Looking down at my son at my breast. What does it matter more than this? Ice on the inside of the window, his body warm against mine.

What does it matter to be remembered? His looking up at me, his eyes. He won't remember. But that moment will do.

Cleaning my desk of ways to be remembered. Yarn to knit a sweater. Pictures of my babies. Beads and silver. Fabric for quilts. Letters and bills and bills and bills.

The rug by the door is stained black from the shoes of the man who repaired the boiler.

HE'S TAKEN HER off of one of her medications. I come home to this. He has told one doctor. Not the one that matters.

There is always laundry when you get home. And things to unpack. The mail keeps coming and trash day comes too. There is ice in the driveway and the sky is gray.

She thinks she has bugs in her fingers and she is picking them out. She is angry. Angry. He's taken her off one of her medications. She is picking them out. I am doing laundry and opening mail.

THURSDAY, FEBRUARY 22

I T IS TUESDAY morning. Tuesday morning always comes. Today when it comes I admit defeat.

This morning came with cold and sun. The house smelling like winter needs to end. Everywhere I look there are more things. More decisions. Apples in a bag left in the car for too long. Frozen and pock-marked. Paper on the floor from hours spent drawing and painting. Mustard-wine sauce in a pan on the stove.

Tuesday morning is a time for reckoning.

The man came a little after ten o'clock. He looked at the heating system. Asked if we had a dishwasher, a garbage disposal. Looked at the box in the basement. I told him the house had won. I admitted defeat. He said it was none of his business.

It is Tuesday morning. In a little while I will try to get the kids out of the house to face Tuesday afternoon. But for now it is still morning. It is Tuesday morning and I admit defeat.

TUESDAY, FEBRUARY 27

QUIET OMENS IN the night. A gate left open. The bone we found in the graveyard. A flag flapping against wrought iron.

Oh, Molly!

While they are talking I am thinking of you.

TUESDAY, MARCH 6

WHEN SHE GOT her Massachusetts license she took it out to show us. She took out his license too. She did it. She copied his smile. She got it right. Her husband, two months gone. She got his smile. Her husband. Hanged.

In the paper there is a letter from Wayne Lo. A letter addressed to the people of a well-to-do place. A letter telling them to remember. That they should have learned. That they should have learned when he killed my friend Galen.

I come home to the house smelling like a burnt-out car. The furnace is gone, running with no water. Cracked. The basement is hot. Nothing catches.

Abigail is better now. Not quite right, but better. Her lungs still making that crinkly noise. Every time she breathes in the tube I think of my father and the things he breathed. I think of my father and his lungs. His lungs.

A stone skips along the surface of the water until it stops and goes under.

JUST GOT HOME and I'm trying not to cry. It's not that there's anything to cry about but sometimes the part of me that is you comes through and I just don't know what to do about it.

I think the old man across the street died today. Old women looking worried, coming and going with their dyed hair. Coming and going all week. And now they've stopped.

The woman in the next house down is on bed rest. So she sits on the front porch smoking cigarettes. Lets the dog out. I don't know how much longer before the baby comes but I'm worried.

I've got that fuzzy feeling in my head like I should be doing more. Or else. Like I should be doing else. Like somebody has decided my decisions aren't right.

I hate them for it.

TUESDAY, APRIL 3

THE SHAPE OF it all coming to me, coming back to me. Pilings rising from the water like the Giant's Causeway. The same thing happens over and over again.

The weather is changing again. Warm air comes in the windows and heats the rooms upstairs. The girls walk down the streets in as little as they can manage. Bass pours out of the cars. The drunks walk home at night. The city breathes with slow breaths, deep, making sure they don't lose their step.

TUESDAY, APRIL 24

I T IS LATE on Monday night and I am up alone. I've got that feeling that I can see everything clearer now. Not intellectually but physically: cigarette butts on the sidewalk, streetlights up above me. I've been thinking of you all week.

It's getting close now. You know how all the rocks have names and all the marshes have mazes. You have always jumped in first while I shivered afraid on the dock. Even the glittering water of Lobster Cove makes me worry I may not come back.

I will turn 31 soon. Prime numbers have treated me well. Things could turn on a dime and I am ready for that but I think I'll go into it with optimism. Tomorrow I will bring my mother and my daughter to the beach and they will look for rocks together. We will choose which beach depending on which life we want to live. We will choose which life we want to live.

The other night I thought the fog horn was a train approaching. Funny how the sounds trade places. It's been years since I've heard a bell buoy. Last week on Front Beach there were pieces of blue beach glass everywhere. Must have been the storm that kicked them up. I haven't told anybody until now.

I had forgotten about irrational numbers but I know they have their place. Days and months and years go by and I don't think of them.

My peas have started to come up. By the time you get back they will have run their course and we will be deep in tomatoes and zucchini. The windows will be open. We will be waiting for you.

A COOL MORNING, rain falling on yesterday's laundry. Last night the air was full of blossoms. It made a kind of mischief in me, like May Day girls dancing in white. It felt like cherry blossoms and cherry blossoms feel like you.

I tried to call you. Dropping Gerrit off as the late-morning sun broke through the rain. Looking back through his jungle, the taste of sorrel in my mouth. The air smelled like rain and earth and rain on earth and I missed you. I dialed your number. That is all that came of it.

BIOGRAPHERS WILL ACCUSE me of trying to reconstruct the people I have lost.

It's all a patchwork.

TIRED FROM THE heat of almost-summer. Windows still shut and fans still away. Afternoon rain in car windows. Baby crying upstairs.

Clean the spiders off of the new bookcase. Clean up puzzles. Move a speaker. Listen to that song. When I go deaf. When I go deaf.

Wash the dishes. Sneak dolls and Teletubbies into the wash. Slip mother's MRI behind the new bookcase. Think of that song. When I go deaf.

Pick up newspapers. Consider gardening at night. Doll's head against the washer. Think about water. Deep water. Hang clothes to dry.

Find a box. Fold a blanket. Try to find things I don't need. When I go deaf.

THESE DAYS THE sun comes up with birds a-twitter and babies crying for the breast. The coffee is hot and the cream is sweet. These days the greens are from the garden. These days the morning dew is just enough to keep the garden happy.

We have jobs to help us buy drinks. We have dryers to pile papers and fabric on. We have babies to sing them to sleep.

Today I may bake a cake with almonds and butter and lemon. I will drink more coffee than I mean to. I will not open the mail.

You ask me what I am looking for.

What can I possibly say?

THERE IS SO little to do when the sky keeps falling. Blue for hours, hang the laundry out. Rain like a curtain, hide away.

There is a game people play when they don't know what to do with themselves. A bit of pin-the-tail-on-the-donkey. Or Operation. Put in the pieces, quickly, where you think you have plastic holes. Don't touch the sides. Don't connect. Hope you don't hit the wall. As if that little plastic femur fills in the empty bits.

Hanging the laundry this morning a green bug fell from the tree above me and landed on my chest. I overreacted. I am sorry for it.

FRIDAY, JUNE 22

GOING TO SEE her the car is faltering, making a grinding noise. Around curves. When braking. The front wheel on my side.

Abby in yesterday's clothes, Sam dressed and smiling. She is crying. Take her in.

Eat together, breaking bread. The waitress pours coffee right over the baby. He ignores her. Too much food, too much to think about.

The car makes it home. Out with the car seats. Out with the carriages. Have it towed.

She is sweeping my rug. Cleaning. Folded laundry, shoes and toys in a box. Keeping busy. Helping.

She dumps my pocketbook into the toy box. Fills it with legos. Rolls it up.

The day goes by.

This is how time is spent.

I AM TRYING to make up with poetry.

Just writing this now seems full of artifice.

If I could have been alone tonight I would have stayed home, picked peas from the garden and sauteed them with ginger.

There is no hope for it.

I can only write love poems.

TUESDAY, JULY 3

TODAY I HAVE to do things my way. I have to have coffee in the morning. Dishes mostly done.

Listen to the same song. Over and over. Empty the baskets she filled and sort them out. Clean laundry in one. Mail on the desk. Plastic cup in the sink.

Monday set me back weeks. Brakes gone. Everything from the car thrown into my sewing room. Feet tired from all the walking.

A month of paper recycling under my desk. I can't miss it again next week. I just can't.

The living room is nearly clean. James is upstairs with a headache. Sam needs a nap. He won't take one.

I will make another cup of coffee. I will vacuum the living room. I will listen to sports radio for comfort. What are we coming to? A meltdown.

WINDING YARN FROM a cone bought unseen, a mistake from years ago. Silk with some wool for good measure. A color called grass. It feels rough like jeans dried on the line. Tough, ropelike on my hands. Trying to wind the perfect ball.

Apple-sized ball and the first knot appears. Break the yarn, start again. Almond-sized for the next knot. Once more, clean start, winding the yarn around my fingers then around itself and around the ball it is becoming. Right arm winding like a machine. Mind of its own. Change the axis. Keep the ball even.

Tired of the burden of product, knitting this time for the process. The pattern comes in bits, weekly, and I don't know what it will be. A stole of some kind. I don't pray. Instead of a prayer shawl I knit memories into each stitch. I can't pray. I remember into each stitch things I hope she won't forget.

Thread on bead. Cast on two stitches. The big glass jar of plastic beads we strung on fishing line, trying to make the longest string of all, up the stairs and onto the bathroom, down the hall and into every room. Knit into the front and back of each stitch. Four stitches. Making eggrolls around the kitchen table, plums and apples bubbling on the stove for a homemade duck sauce. Knit the next row. Driving down 133 in the old Singer to the White Lion. Galen throwing a piece of kielbasa with tamari out the window.

Knit one. Place bead. The birthday party after my father left. Me in my

Chinese outfit, sick with the throw bug. All adults except for two girls my age. I wanted a cocktail party. Yarn over. A bowl of cheese curls. Place bead. Knit one.

Knit two, purl to last two stitches, knit two. All even rows. The smell of a bathroom filled with coffee and cigarette smoke. Follow the chart carefully. Kids lining up for her tremendous chocolate chip cookies, no recipe, each the size of a hockey puck. All the teeth lost in those cookies. Keep the first and last two stitches in each wrong-side row in garter stitch.

The dresses she made me. Lines of yarn overs climbing the edges of the stole. Swimming in the waves after hurricanes. Legs raw from the barnacles on the rocks. Place a bead on the center stitch.

Yarn rough on my hands, the melon-sized ball showing no signs of shrinking. Following the chart carefully, trying hard not to get any of the memories wrong.

SUNDAY, JULY 8

T UESDAY MORNING AGAIN. It always seems to come. The babies are coughing, doctor in the afternoon.

Find a hammer. Do all the chores that need a hammer. Fix the curtain rod. Pound a loose nail.

If I had twenty minutes I would pull the dried peas out of the garden. I would water the plants. Pick flowers.

Find a pen. Do all the chores that need a pen. Thank you notes. Bills. Make a list of things to do.

If I had twenty minutes I would piece together a picture of fabric. Black and white and red. Like I am thinking of you. Right angles and spirals. Black and white.

Turn the computer on. Do all the chores that require a computer. Check email. Reply to friends. Waste time.

If I had twenty minutes I would tell the birds stories that would make them grow teeth to bite the stones from cherries.

T HESE DAYS I am baking scones for neighbors. Making whales of old fabric. Saving bottle caps and pull tabs.

Sunday morning the sun rose first like a pink ghost then orange with a red halo and finally bright and bold and yellow. I am making stories out of hellos and goodbyes and writing middles where nothing was before.

I am making myself giddy with thin air.

Today I locked my keys in the car and breathed reconditioned air. I ate bland food and sat through idle chatter. I bought diapers and fabric and buttons and bug spray. I didn't care through all of it because I am using my imagination. I am making characters to suit my needs.

They gather little bits of quiet exuberance and try to build a life of it.

TUESDAY, JULY 31

T HERE ARE SO many people to think of in a day. Looking through her things, trying to get them in some order. Piecing together her story.

In a plastic bag her silver beads are held together by white acrylic paint, the tube left open. And the earrings I bought her in Cobh. A tin painted with enamels, black with green dots and a white dove. An olive branch. Old bank statements and lots of socks, covered in dog hair, never matching. Glittery gold tights.

A closet full of raw silk scraps. Each color in its own bag, each bag used before for something else. Rusts and browns bagged together. A bag of black the size of a laundry basket, baby blue the size of a loaf of bread. For years her palette, somebody else's scraps. Hours spent cutting and ironing and piecing together. I pack the bags in plastic bins to be put in storage and probably never seen again.

I couldn't take it home.

Pictures from my freshman year of high school, hair long and blonde, next to a boy who loved me. He spent hours sunbathing in my driveway, talking to the neighbors, waiting for me to come home. Brought me to watch the sun rise. Waited for me for hours.

Anne Marie across the street sees me and calls me in. She has had a dress in her hallway closet for twenty years. Purple gingham. Made by my mother, worn by my sister, then me, then her daughter. She gives it to me for Abby. The finishing is perfect.

Today Sam took four steps. It should be noted.

TONIGHT I AM killing flies. They have taken over the kitchen. Little fruit flies landing on the sink and the cabinets and the mirror my grandfather's uncle made. I have cleaned everything: the sink, the dish drain, the pitcher from on top of my grandmother's piano. I have set glasses of wine all over the kitchen. Quarter-full of old white wine, a drop of dish soap in each. Poisoned wine for unwanted guests.

There is so much to go through. Satin ribbon, rickrack, embroidery floss and piping all jumbled together. Rayon seam binding. Hundreds of zippers. I try my best to sort it out, untangle the ends. I will never use all these zippers. It is impossible to know which ones I will.

In the back of the car is a trash bag full of jingle bells. Hundreds and thousands of jingle bells. You should hear the sound they make.

She came back from California and spent the next day in bed not eating or drinking. When we saw her she looked thin. She was shaking. Even the kids couldn't make her smile.

By the next day she was fine.

I AM TRYING hard not to be in a bad mood right now. I came home from a few days away to find my computer broken. It won't start. Won't turn on. I think it is a problem of power but who the hell knows. Oddly enough there is an extra computer here, slower and messier, lacking all content the broken one has.

It makes me sad, this losing things.

Picking raspberries in Lancaster I was thinking about my grandmother. I wanted to sing a song for her. I sang the song that made me sad after she died. I sang the song I sang at her service. Neither worked. As raspberries fell off the bushes into my hands I tried to think of a song she loved as much as she loved her raspberries. Nothing came. I started to sing the song I sang when my grandfather remarried. I felt like a traitor.

This keyboard makes different mistakes than my own. When does a house take over? Their house was always filled with his music. Even what she liked was his. I know she loved Bergman films and watching tennis and seeing schoolchildren when they were abroad. I can't think of one song that was hers.

I am in a sour mood and it is hard to explain. Even to myself. Sam has climbed the stairs and will cry when I get him. Maybe if I do something good I will feel better. Bake muffins for the neighbors. All the stories in my new book were sad about love. I'm beginning to think that's all the Irish write about: sad love.

Maybe I'll do something bad. Bake little unzipped gingermen. Serve them with whiskey and fuck it all.

HARD TO GET up in the morning. Head groggy, noggy groggy, groggy noggin. Morning shower, telephone call, unexpected progress and unexpected bliss.

My mother was resting in the sunlight when I went in to get her. Her dogs were at her feet.

We were wasting time, sunlight on us, driving around and stopping where we could. At the Chinese restaurant we waited outside for the food to be done, singing songs together. Oh, don't you cry for me. Little bits of love finding their way in.

Across the parking lot the man I feared for years and years was talking to a ward councilor. He stopped to wave to me. I waved back.

Beautiful hangover day.

TUESDAY, AUGUST 14

TONIGHT I AM despondent, quiet in the face of it. Days go by and I can ignore the way things are, the way they will be.

I thank every one of you who distracts me.

There is a rash on her side, a sore on her face. One is caused by bugs crawling out of her skin. The other is from blood dripping out of her ear. I recommend a bandage and a cotton dress. More time spent looking for heart-shaped rocks, less time wandering around rooms alone.

There is a pit in my stomach, an empty feeling in my head. I'm going to try a drink.

S HE WAS WELL on Sunday, a ride for coffee and to look at the water.

On Monday a morning visit to give her her pills. She had made coffee herself. After Sam's appointment we went again, this time a ride to Newburyport. Lunch at the diner. A little walk around. A ride to Plum Island.

Tuesday morning, her birthday, a quick get-ready then coffee with her father. A card with a picture of her as a girl holding her baby sister, now dead. She doesn't cry. She didn't sleep well, thunder and all. Has a hard time following conversation.

Wednesday morning and she is tired. She can't sleep without him, where is he? I explain again: He'll be home soon. Coffee with her aunt and uncle. She can't find her words. Stutters. Says the wrong things. Sam, just walking, keeps stumbling into Bernie's paintings. Left out for an agent to look at later. By the time we leave she doesn't make sense but she is comfortable. You can hear it in her voice.

I bring her to her friend's house. Stopping in the art store the man asks how she is, if she's better. He's known her for years. And I tell him no, she's not better. She is not going to get better. I pay for my paper and leave.

That evening I bring her to the hospital to meet her newest grandchild. She manages the crowd, laughs at the wrong times. She is quiet on the way home.

This is how our hearts break. We watch the people we love hurt and nobody can say a thing.

I AM LOOKING for self-confidence this morning.

I can't say quite what it is, quite why it is. A pile of fabric scraps on the kitchen floor. Chicken that should be cooked tonight. But there is something wavering about the day, a little breeze of uncertainty.

Maybe it is because I can't really read you. Or that the weed whacker is broken. Or that yesterday's mail sits unopened. I feel like I've been giving too much away.

I still want to open the windows to the morning air.

IT'S FUNNY, TONIGHT, how much I want to talk to someone. I wish I could talk on the phone. I wish I had something to say.

I meant to tell you about my long day last week. The phone call in the morning asking me to call if my mother died. Crying in the tunnel over everything lost. Bringing the kids to Boston Medical to see Other Grammie with her broken neck. Parking on the top floor just to see the sky. Red Jello spilled all over the car. Lunch at Real Taco with a funeral on TV. An hour and a half of traffic on the way home. Counting at the supermarket. Risotto with mushrooms and caramelized onions and spinach. Salmon with mustard dill sauce. Driving the kids to sleep.

It struck me that day, watching the people come and go. People in uniforms, people in hospital beds, people in cars, how odd it is that we love the people we love. That frail man in the next bed. The driver of the truck that cut me off. The older woman talking to me in line. How funny it is that with a different twist of fate they could be the people I love.

TUESDAY, SEPTEMBER 11

I T HAD BEEN a good day. The kind of day that makes you wonder why sometimes it is so hard. The kind of day that makes you think you are good. And then it happened. Nothing major, a run-in with the recycling man, about what numbers mean, number two and number six.

I have been wrong. For months I have been putting plastic bags and styrofoam in my bin. I believed the numbers. I should have known better.

My horoscope warned me about this, about being comfortable. On the way to the park I couldn't get coffee. I couldn't get a styrofoam cup I couldn't recycle.

What else am I doing that is wrong?

Cleaning the living room this evening I came out from under my desk to find myself staring at the spider with seven legs. I must have cut his line from the ceiling. I didn't want him there but days ago I had decided that he, with his seven legs, had the right to live on my ceiling. I didn't know what to do.

I got up to put a bowl in the sink. A sock in the hamper.

When I came back he was gone.

WEDNESDAY, SEPTEMBER 19

I CAN'T STOP thinking of those children watching their mother die. Waiting as her body slowly gives up. Remembering my father as his body stopped working. Watching the pieces go.

Sitting at Nina's counter, her feeding me cookies and pouring me tea. Talking about our lives, our families. Her children doing well, playing music, applying for school. Mine still in my belly.

Potatoes were on sale yesterday at the market. Buy one bag get two free. Spinach too, buy one and get one free. We'll be having spinach-oatmeal soup soon, and shepherd's pie. Potatoes roasted with salt and pepper and rosemary from the garden if I can find any.

I wonder if her family came, if they figured it out.

Yesterday's spider came back, crawling up the kitchen cabinet this morning. Up and down with his seven legs. Abigail didn't want him there. Wanted to use a napkin to shoosh him away. Instead I caught him in a cup and left him outside.

Nina's copy of *Bartok for Children* is still on my piano. The spine taped where I said I would fix it.

I will bake something to leave there at their door. I can't expect them to get it. I can't expect it will matter.

There is love we put into things. We can never get it back.

THURSDAY, SEPTEMBER 20

THE THING ABOUT letting everything go to seed is that the birds love it. They hop about the yard, past the mustard and the thistle. The whole thing is a place to hide.

Reading translations in the tub after everyone else is asleep. I'm not sure where I fit into it all, the elbows and the wool. But the peace of it.

I have been ignoring my mother lately. That is not true. What I should say is that sometimes when I wake at night I let myself think of something else and I am happy.

I CALLED THIS morning to tell her I would be late. Just after noon. When I got there she was upset. She didn't know where I was. It continued like that today. Missed cues, little complications. Typical for a Tuesday.

There are things I want from a Monday. Sometimes they come, sometimes not. I have no right to them but I want them just the same. A little music to dance to, some Monday night words. The best I got last night was reading *My Vote Counts* to a most offensive mayoral candidate.

Sometimes these days of the week have minds of their own.

TUESDAY, OCTOBER 2

WHEN THE MORMONS come I don't know what to do with them. So I teach them how to knit. They sit with the kids while I look for yarn. They pick shiny metal needles from my extras. They chose colors.

I cast on for them. They are nervous. They fumble with the wool and it slides all over the place.

The quiet one gets it right away. Her hands know what to do. The one who talks about blessings and the prophet and the book is having a hard time. Her stitches are tight. She splits the yarn.

I ask them what they are doing. Four hours of service a week. They came to my house to weed-whack my lawn and I start them knitting hats for Afghans. They ask if I was raised in a church. I ask why circumstances of class and connections are called blessings.

The quiet one finishes a row. She says something thoughtful every so often. The one who talks has trouble with her tight stitches. She keeps returning to the book. She tells me about rules and blessings. About following laws even if you don't know them. I talk to them about anarchy and *Jane Eyre*.

I lend them a book of knitting instructions. I know they will be back to return it. The one who talks asks me to write down my questions so she can research them. She says she's no genius. They leave me with the *Book of Mormon*. With passages to read.

They say I must be obedient to have the blessing of my home and children.

They have no idea.

WEDNESDAY, OCTOBER 3

EVERY TIME I have to tell someone it becomes new again. When I say it I can see the parts of her brain going away. The dark spots on the scan. When they start to cry I cry too.

Tomorrow when the Mormons come back to talk to me about heaven I will ask them. Is there a place in heaven for the parts of a person that go away?

O N   T H E   WAY to the doctor she says she is going to throw up. She is wringing her hands. She says she is going to be bad.

She has new buttons on her jacket. Buttons all over the front. Where the top button should be is a string of five or six buttons that jingle when she walks. There are buttons on the side with button holes. Silver and gold, silver and gold. One with a pearl center. She has sewn antique buttons all over the front of her jacket.

When we get to the door she starts to run away. I grab her, hold her. She screams at me and tries to shake her way out. The buttons on her jacket jingle. She frees her arms and swings at me. Let me go let me go no way no way no way. I hold her again and tell her I love you mom I love you. She is crying.

I ask her if she remembers last year. She doesn't. I tell her how dark it was. How she couldn't talk or paint or sew. How she wanted to die. I ask her if she is happy now. She says yes. She lets me bring her in.

When the Mormons came this week they tried to answer my questions by the book. They told me I need the milk before the meat. They sat and knit and let me ask about celestial marriage and sexism and the spirit mother. We talked about love and god. In trying to tell me that love is god the talking one read a passage that made me an antichrist. She was so sad when I pointed it out.

Before they left they sang a song for me and said a prayer for my mother.

Inside the doctor's office she is mad and she is crying and she says no no no. She doesn't want to be there. She won't let him touch her. By the end she has answered his questions. She is mostly quiet. She is resigned.

Driving down Washington Street bringing her home she says I take good care of her. She says she loves me. She says thank you.

T HE HOUSE IS cold again, today like yesterday and the day before. I won't turn the heat on.

An hour at the market and at the end of it the fear of not being able to pay. Electrical glitch last week, expected money absent all weekend. I packed the cold things together in case my card didn't work. Crossed fingers. It did.

Leeks from Friday at Appleton Farm and potatoes from last week's sale on the stove. Everything I do gets quickly undone and I do it again. All day this way. Clean up the blocks. Sweep the floor. Fold laundry. Repeat.

I'm listening to songs I shouldn't bother listening to. They fit the futility of the day. Only recently familiar and already like old friends.

The sheets are in the wash. This is recycling week. The soup on the stove is warming the kitchen a little and there's coffee almost ready to drink. I might slip away and ignore the whole thing.

If you think I'm crying for you today you are less than half right.

MONDAY, OCTOBER 15

WAKING UP EVERY morning to the price of oil rising. The sunflowers outside have all turned brown. The birds are making the most of them.

Everything is one step away from desperation.

THE DAY IS half-way done and I am starting to slow. We are drinking tea to stay warm. We are remembering how to layer our clothing.

Around every corner there's another thing to do. Trying to keep up with it, trying to be productive. I have a picture in my mind and I doubt I'll get to it.

I am holding my head high. Trying to find value in matching socks. I'll have to turn the heat on soon.

S TEPPING OUTSIDE THIS morning it feels like spring. The birds singing in the bushes, a lightness in the air, a new crop of peas coming up in the pot by the stairs.

We are dancing in the kitchen, a baby on each hip, singing in full voice. We are eating root vegetables and ripe pears.

I am remembering how important it is to hear your name spoken out loud.

OUTSIDE ON THE smoking deck blues inside and they're joking show it they say and he lifts his shirt under his arm the tattoo the numbers sniper's numbers and I can't help but think of what they mean what sniper means what marines means and I say something about peace and go inside and I am standing there standing my eyes are tearing and an older man talks to me tries to cheer me up tells me not to change the world not to try and says it's okay but I'm thinking about numbers and snipers and murder and death and I'm thinking about babies and children and parents and I'm thinking about parents and dead children and death and I'm crying and the band is playing and the whiskey's gone and I'm crying I go outside I go back outside and talk to him and he's fine it's okay and I'm crying about number and dead children and he knows he agrees and he shows me a picture of his boy twelve years old and he talks about war and about being young and about politics and love and green energy and in the end we're talking about Colorado and the weather and in the end we are talking about baseball.

T ODAY EVERYBODY IS tired. Our feet are sore from standing in lines. Our babies are grumpy from lack of sleep.

We are the lucky ones.

HARD THIS WEEK, the days of it all together with the days that have come before them. Those two houses. They make me remember. Standing in line for hours. Looking at bodies and trinkets. The delirious feeling after hours in one room. Saying I'm sorry and hearing I'm sorry and being sorry. The way faces all look the same. The way make-up cakes at the edge of a bullet hole.

SATURDAY, OCTOBER 27

WATER MAIN BROKEN downtown. No laundry, no dishes. No baths for the kids. The water's brown. So dirty it leaves a ring in the bathroom sink. I can't make coffee.

At the market my mother tries to talk to everyone. She mistakes their wanting her to move her carriage for a more pleasant eye contact. She doesn't understand.

At the check-out the man looks at each thing. Says its name. Says its size. 28 ounce can of Kitchen Ready tomatoes. Rings it in. Looks at the computer and reads what it says. 28 ounces. Kitchen Ready tomatoes. Artichokes. Oats-and-More cereal. Market Basket shredded cheddar cheese. Martin's potato bread.

It is the longest check-out. Sam is crying. My mother puts him on the conveyor belt. He is happy. I bag my groceries as they come down. The man doesn't turn the second belt on and I have to reach for the tomatoes and the cereal and the cheese.

My mother is minding Sam. She doesn't put her groceries up. By the time I notice this a man behind her has his out, blue divider between his and mine. I pick Sam up and put her food where he was.

The man puts a pen in front of Sam. He picks it up. He gives Sam the receipt to sign. The man looks at my groceries and wants to bag the rest.

Sam is crying again. I ask the man to please ring her food in. He wants to bag. I ask again. I promise I can keep them separate. He yields. By the time he is done naming her food it is almost all bagged. He tells her the total: $43. She only has $40. My card is already in my bag beneath the groceries. I dig it out. Take her $40. Pay for her food.

On the way home we stop for a cup of coffee. She digs in her purse for money to pay for it. I tell her it's my turn.

DRIVING HOME IN the midnight light, stars bright above us and the moon a yellow shock behind Stage Fort. Every other car is a cab or a cop. Drive through the Fort, to find the moon again.

My city at night. It is quieter after I drop Jane off, up over Beacon Street and onto Washington. The cabs are driving like there are no lines and the streets are empty. The night shines down on City Hall. On Main Street. On the steamy laundromat on Maplewood Ave.

I miss you.

T RYING TO GET back to it, to get my wits about me. Today the snow and the rain fell around me and landed like crystals and tears.

I can't remember when I stopped singing my lover to sleep.

A LITTLE HEARTBROKEN today. The tone of my mother's voice. The girl at the bar Monday night. The way parts of the house feel cold even with the heat on.

I have been spending my days making things for other people to buy. I have been working until my fingers are sore.

It is another form of love: letting these things that are a part of me go.

MY HOUSE IS filled with balloons. The kitchen cabinet is falling off of the wall. My living room is filled with fabric from another of my mother's closets.

Today she watched Sam while I put parts of her life in boxes and into my car. She sat him on the counter and fed him pieces of bagel. She gave him an antique doll to play with. And when her dog snapped at him she pulled Sam up quickly and cried with him.

She cried and was sorry and couldn't talk. She wandered around and couldn't find her things and cried and said she was sorry. I told her not to worry. Everything is fine.

I would lie through my teeth to make her happy.

TODAY IT IS difficult not to drink. I mean not to drink early. This morning with ice over everything and no cream for coffee, like a sign or something that whiskey would do or bourbon or scotch or anything but coffee with no cream.

There is a smell in the house, a bad smell, like lost sippy cup or worse. Keep doing laundry. Close the gate upstairs and mop the floor. Replace the bad smell with the bad smell of bleach. Strip the beds.

Wash Sam's chair. Scrub yogurt from the grooves in the table. Bring the garbage outside. Knock the ice off the lid. Shovel the steps, the walk. Throw salt on it.

Watch the crows fly away. I forgot about winter, the way things have of freezing shut. The way Windex freezes on a window.

At one o'clock Jane brings me cream. I give her soup. I set oranges and cloves to boil on the stove.

It is after noon and I haven't had a drink.

My streak stands unbroken.

I T'S FEELING LIKE a hot stove life these days. I don't know who to talk to. I don't know who to trade.

I'm waiting for the Mitchell Report to blow it all up.

THURSDAY NIGHT A mind of its own with snow and cold and no dinner and too much bourbon. There will be mistakes and I'm sorry for them but it's the way it is. There are always mistakes.

So it's Thursday and it's blues night and we end up out, out with Shilo's brother, and eventually I'll call him Ryan but not tonight and the music's okay but loud and the night is ending and in comes Mac and he sits with us of course he sits with us and the music is ending and I let him buy us drinks because the night is nearly over and his wife is dead and I was thinking about her Sunday and we have whiskey and I dance with Mac because he is lonely.

And the music ends and we sit down and we talk and Dave Sag comes up and Dave knows Gregor I'm his right-hand-man and Dave knows Anne Marie and Dave came to Gloucester after her. And it is December 13th heading into December 14th and Dave tells me he held Galen in his arms when he was a baby and it is December 14th and I make Mac get me another drink and it is December and Dave knew Anne Marie when she was baking bread and I baked for Mac and it is December 14th Dave held Galen in his arms and I will remember that this morning when my baby wakes up I will remember Anne Marie wailing in my kitchen as her baby lay dead in Great Barrington.

And it is Thursday night and I haven't eaten and we are talking about Galen and Gloucester and Anne Marie and Mac says out of nowhere that he misses my father and hell I miss my father and we drink to that but I'm the only one drinking and I am a Lacey and Dave talks about my mother and he remembers her and she doesn't even remember herself. I drink to that. And the night ends and I stumble home in the snow and I reheat leftover spaghetti and I've had too much to drink but I love you and I miss you and this morning it is fifteen years and nearly four years and who knows when my mother started to lose it but I love you I love you all.

FRIDAY, DECEMBER 14

CHRISTMAS NIGHT THE day long and gone and a lot of good in it. Plastic toys rattle in the back of the car. Sam cries as we sit in traffic.

I am trying to keep the tender parts of me tender.

Pickup truck rolled over. Car smashed in. A peace in knowing she would not be alone. The rising of a voice brings me to tears. The way we light things up and call them joy.

I ask if I am doing all I can. Am I doing all I can?

TWO DAYS AFTER Christmas and the emergency room is full. She didn't know what she was doing, a week's worth of pills. Forty-two pills. A week's worth.

In the next room a man has taken something and fallen off of a fishing boat. He is cold. He screams for two hours while they try to figure out his name. Down the hall a little girl is so sick they send her straight to Children's. An old woman wanders from room to room doing EKGs.

We watch as her heart speeds up and slows down. We wait to be moved. A woman with chest pains sits and waits alone. A man with a blown-out knee waits on a stretcher.

The next day when I go to the hospital to visit I find a slide on the wet pavement. The corner of the Public Garden by Beacon and Arlington. The corner I sat in so many times. The edge of the statue shows and I remember what it says. Neither shall there be any more pain.

2008

O ATMEAL FOR BREAKFAST. Kids are coughing, just a little, into the tub and out to play. Pull on torn jeans and slip on heels to mail a letter.

Cut tomatoes and fresh mozzarella, basil and olive oil into bread. Stale crackers onto the porch for the birds. Dance around the kitchen. Hang the upstairs rug to dry. Still finding beer bottles and glasses of bourbon and grappa and eggnog and wine. Bags of Waragi and plates of chocolates.

Kiss the kids as they run through and send them up to play. Reheat coffee. This year I will live the way I mean to. Make better use of my resources. Write more letters.

This year I will act out of love.

HE'S GONE AWAY for a week. She is upset about it, about being alone without him. So we make sure she is not alone. We write our names on a calendar. We commit to time. Each day we will check on her, see her, make sure she is not alone.

Today I take her to get coffee. In her purse is a large container of organic yogurt. She puts it on the table at the cafe. She pulls out a white shirt with a black stain. She is going to fix it, she says. Then I can have it. It will be as good as new. She trips on her words. They come out sideways.

When Sam makes eyes at a little girl my mother tells a man it is love in place. Nobody cares that her words are wrong. Nobody is listening.

A T THE CAFE a woman sits with her back to me talking to the photographer. He tells her the story of each picture and as he is talking I can imagine what each one is. The bow cutting across the water. The gravestones. The buildings.

My mother is late. I drink more coffee than I should waiting for her. Sam eats cream cheese off of a bagel. He reads a book.

When she gets there she is all aflutter. Bags of canvases and paints. I get her a cup of coffee. I get her rye toast. We work on her homework: lists of things, categories. Lists of how to do things. We go to her house. As she learns how to find her words Sam crawls under the table, around the chairs. By the time we are done he is covered in dog hair.

We drive downtown doing this week's homework. How a fence is different from a wall. How they are the same.

When I pick Abigail up she is holding an invisible baby bird in her hands. She asks us to be quiet so the baby bird can sleep. By the time we get home the baby bird is awake. She lifts her hands out of the car door and lets it fly away.

WHAT I READ as a hangover this morning turns out to be something else. Getting sick. A cough, a headache. A tightness in my lungs. I can feel it like a train coming.

Words and pictures. We put them everywhere. When I say I love you, you think I am selling you soap.

AFTERNOON AND I am waiting for snow. I am full after eating the way you eat to get someone else to eat. As if it were charity.

I am trying to decide what in my life I have control over. What is a choice. Instead of sitting here letting it all wash over me.

I T IS SPRING. There are plants in the garden. I am cooking dinner. The kids are upstairs playing. The air is cool.

I am trying to start a new story. But the story stays the same.

WE ARE STARTING over.

Every day we wake up to a new light, a new chance, a new hope.

Every day is dashed to the ground like the days before it.

MONDAY, JULY 21

QUIET MORNING NAKED in bed tired-eyed knitting and listening and still. Cat on the covers lists of things to do lists and lists and things to do. Up into yesterday's jeans. Out into the old truck. Coffee in the sunshine morning. Yardsaling. Finding friends. Old glass buoys and clock cabinets.

I have wasted the day. Wonderful wasted day.

TODAY SHE HAS lost her glasses. Athena from down the street is there with a flashlight looking for them. Athena who doesn't get it. Athena who keeps asking her to retrace her steps. We leave without her glasses. Athena stays to make herself a cup of coffee.

MONDAY NIGHT HOME from the bar and I'm awake and I'm tired. Dance music tonight but the floor was too full too crowded and I didn't want to fight my way up didn't want to dance in back. Girls with plucked eyebrows and tattooed backs and I can't shake the feeling I'm not being the person I mean to be.

Do you remember that time you came out to my bar? I just remembered it, just now.

Tonight a cab ride home never done that before and I'm not even drunk, not even tired. I wasn't dancing for anyone tonight even when the kids came. I could eat something now if there was something to eat, or call someone if I liked the phone. I am home and I don't even know if the Phillies won the World Series.

T**UESDAY**, O**CTOBER** 2 8

2009

L AUNDRY TO BE folded in the new year, laundry and dishes and more of the same. My glasses are broken and they need to be fixed.

I have thirty dollars in the pocket of a pair of dirty jeans and I swear I am going to find it.

WALKING BEHIND HIM on the way to the train. A list of Ians in my head. The one who lost himself out west. The one who had sword fights in Glasgow and heroin here.

Thinking about the way men smell when they work. This one smells like wood. That one smells like stale cigarette sweat. The way men smell when they move things.

I am trying to notice things again.

S PRING IS TURNING to somewhere and everywhere I turn there is new growth. The peas are coming out from behind the blossoms. The radishes need to be thinned.

I am going to make this work.

C LEANING THE FRIDGE for soup. Losing time here and there and here again. Cucumbers in jar with dill from Gerrit. Piles of things to do. Sam in his pajamas. We are moving along.

2010

T IME FOR BED and the kids are tired of the songs I am singing. Think hard reach back my funny valentine goin' down the road quiet nights may there always be sunshine. There's a lot to do, not getting it done. Stomach hurts. Virgina Woolf in the tub then off to bed.

TUESDAY MORNING AND the poppies are out. The air is hot and the world is noisier with the windows open. Yesterday's geraniums in the ground, last week's lilies still unplanted. Bird-song all around.

FEELING HUMAN TODAY. Cool air coming in the windows. Potato leek soup on the stove. Tomatoes cooked and peeled and in the freezer, more in a salad with basil and garlic. Watermelon cut.

The week in a blur: mother fall emergency room call sit wait shoulder pain out blood sit. Drive Kingston kids home hospital home sleep hospital drive kids home hospital work. Out home sleep hospital wait hospital wait hold mother cry hold mother. Repeat. Wait. Listen. Cry again. Out into the sun for a moment. Sleep. Hospital. Bring her home. Try to make her happy again.

Late-summer harvest: holding my mother as she tries to take the clothes off my back so she can get out into the sun.

TODAY EVERYTHING FEELS like a punishment.

Sitting at my kitchen table, big tears rolling down her cheeks, big tears rolling onto my arms and dripping onto the floor. I get the softest napkin we have to dry her face. Hold her head to my bosom and dry her tears.

He wants her to have a baby, she thinks. In the shed she has an antique hospital bed, an antique crib for babies. He wants her to have a baby and she can't do it. She counts her babies. One, two, three, four. She counts ten babies. It is too much. She flicks her hands. Sh-sh-sh—her babies are all gone.

She is done with them.

THURSDAY, SEPTEMBER 30

2011

QUIET DAY, FIRST of the new year, kids and James out for a walk. Snow-melt dripping outside. Thankful for a chance at starting anew.

SATURDAY, JANUARY 1

I AM TRYING to decide why I am so heartbroken.

The house is quiet, save for the dripping of the kitchen sink and the heat going on every so often. I am hungry and I may eat a cheese sandwich. I spent hours in the tub reading a book from my oldest friend. When it was done I washed my face and my arms and my chest.

Now I am here. The house is cold the way sitting feels cold. The way being still freezes over. There is something in this being cold and quiet and hungry in a still house. I am sitting here. I am trying to decide why I am so heartbroken.

THIS WEEK SHE laughed and she cried and she pulled my hair. When it was raining she rubbed her legs. When she found strands of fake pearls she wanted me to turn them into money. When I fed her she ate happily.

She hums now. All day, humming. Yesterday I could hear the song. Down in the valley. After she hummed for an hour I sang the words for her. After I sang for an hour she sang some of the words. Angels in heaven. Know I love you.

HARD ARRIVAL EARLY crying running into the car and running away try to get food for her get food into her but she runs away again and my children are crying now crying as I hold her from running away. Back to her house tv on she sits and sits then cries again runs upstairs holds on holds on to the banister screaming screaming about her four dead babies and my children follow up Abby is crying about the babies and my mother won't move can't move screaming holding on on the top stair and I hold her keep her safe tell my children it's okay it's okay and I ease her up off the stairs into the room at the top onto the chair and my children come to her they hold her hand she can breathe now breath again and the babies she talks about the babies and my children tell her it's okay. I bring them back downstairs run back up to her standing in the room talking gibberish to the mirror until she says in plain English "We're nuts."

TUESDAY, APRIL 19

ONE THING I never expected anyone to say to me:

I will say a rosary. You go upstairs and get a diaper on your mom.

THURSDAY, MAY 5

I T IS RAINING. She is upset when I get there. A tooth has broken off. When we ask if there is any pain she says no but every time her tongue finds the spot she cries out about her tooth. Like someone has stolen it. Her tooth.

I change the subject. Get her coffee. She finds two paintings and carries them around, yelling that they are hers. She made them. When she finds her tooth missing again she runs out of the room screaming about her tooth. She cries in the mirror. Runs to my little boy. Bending down in front of him she yells "I am not a person. I am not a person."

When she is calm enough I get her into the car. We have three and a half hours to spend and I won't spend them that way, her yelling at my little boy. I ask if we should drive north or south. Nobody answers. I pick north. Trying to find some old memory I say we are going to Building 19. We drive far, too far, still not far enough. It has been so long and I can't find it anymore. My memory fails me and I drive through Georgetown without remembering which way to go. I drive through Groveland. I turn into West Newbury and into Newburyport. Sam is tired and hungry. My mother slips in and out of sleep. Sam sleeps as we cross 95.

I ask my mother if she wants coffee. She nods. Two cups at a McDonald's window and I turn to drive back home. Nearing downtown Newburyport she takes a sip and I don't know what happened. She couldn't swallow it. Didn't swallow it. She explodes, her head hanging down then up again another explosion. She has no idea what is happening. I pull over, grab a blanket from the back and calm her as I try to brush the vomit off of her. She is whimpering. I tell her it is okay. I always tell her it is okay. We are a long way from home. As I drive she looks straight forward like a blind woman.

I get back into town. Find a place for Sam. I get her home and upstairs. Try to get her into the tub but she won't. She won't she won't she won't she won't. I leave the room and try again. I can't undress her. She yells at me, tells me I am jealous. Calls me her mother. I step out of the room and come back again as her daughter. She is crying and for a moment understands that she needs to get clean. Because she was sick. She is not bad. She agrees for the moment but before I can get her into the tub she is angry again. I leave the room twice more before she gets in the tub.

Clean now I find some clothes for her, dress her and get her warm. She seems to want to go to bed but won't climb in. Something clicks and she is angry again. She finds her bag and holds it like riot police hold shields. Keeping it between her and me, using it to move me back. We go from room to room. At the top of the stairs she tells me to get out. She says she will kill me. I change the subject. Get her looking for shoes. Downstairs a few minutes later she is hissing at me to get out. I plead with her like I am sixteen again. Like she is my mother. It does no good.

TUESDAY IS A hard day. Everywhere we go she runs away from me. Even when we go to walk the on the beach she runs away. Up the hill, fast enough that it is hard to catch her. When I do she says no and hits my hand away. Runs again when I get her to the car.

We drive into the village to pick Sam up. He is with a friend. My mother comes with me, out of the car. When she sees the kids and the other mother she says no again and makes her way over the rocks to a corner of the yard. She scutters around until she finds a way out. When I try to get her into the car she swings at me and runs away, down toward the road. I try to turn her around without touching her. I back her up to the car. She starts to run again and I grab her, hug her around her arms. She swings at me. Hits my forearms and anything else she can reach. She yells at me, calls me Fat Face. The other mother doesn't know what to do. She gets Sam into the car as I hold my mother.

We are near the car. I hold her, move her over, until she is at the front seat. When I tell her this is the way to get away she concedes and gets into the car. I buckle her in, close the door. Before I can get in the driver's seat she is out again. This continues. Five times I have to get her in the car. The other mother holds the door shut until I get in. I drive away.

I don't talk. Sam doesn't talk. My mother doesn't make a sound. As we leave the village she tries to open the car door. I say no, she stops. She keeps trying as we drive home. As we wait at the last set of lights she tries once more. I have to lean over to stop her.

Now when I show up she says "No, not you." She sees me and runs out the door. If I talk she scrunches up her nose and says "Aren't you sweet?" She calls me You or Fat Face. I sit around the corner, trying not to talk, listening to make sure she is safe. When she goes for the door I stop her. I try not to let her see me. Not to look at her. She stares at me with the hate mothers reserve for their daughters. I try not to talk.

WEDNESDAY, JUNE 15

C OOL THIS MORNING. Still feeling the chill of last
night's rain. The wind whipping the flames of the fire downtown.
I feel turned around.

WANDERING IN A haze, trying to find a place to be. Everything I touch has a history of its own. Each room filled, full of the past. Me stuck in the middle. In piles. My children will be home soon. I will find comfort in their needing me.

THURSDAY, OCTOBER 13

2012

FRIDAY MORNING, BOUND by the rain, waiting for the house to warm. The last of the coffee, a bit of last night's dinner. Too many nights out and it shows.

TODAY SHE SAID my name.

She hasn't said my name in a long time. I said my name and then she said my name. It could have been any name. It was my name.

SHE HAD ANOTHER seizure. Four in the morning. She fell this time, hard, on her face. By the time I find out she is at the nursing home again. When they tell me she is asleep.

When I get there she is up. Standing. She won't open her eyes. She grabs my arm, my breast, pulls at my jeans. I say I'm here. It's okay. She grabs at the bandage above her eye. Pulls at the stitches. Her hand is bloody and her head is bloody and I pull her to me. I hold her to my chest and tell her it's alright. She turns and walks into the wall. She can't open her eyes. She is crying.

She starts to sit where she is. I hold her, ease her to the floor. Ease her back up again. She hums and cries and cries and hums. She can't see where she is and I tell her I love her. I love her. She is pinching my middle and grabbing me she puts her arm in my shirt and through my bra strap and she pulls into me. I whisper to her. Hold her. Ease her down into her blue chair and cover her with a blanket. Put her head back. Walk her to sleep.

I watch her sleep. The blood drying into her eyebrow. The bruise on her forehead. The faint stain on the pillow from the blood in her wet hair. When she wakes she wants to walk right away. I take one arm. L. takes the other. She is woozy and we hold her up. She still can't open her eyes. She still cries. I tell her the lights are out. I tell her we're okay. They give her something for pain. I try to give her vanilla ice cream. They give her something to make her rest and she fights it she fights it she walks and pushes and cries and fights but she can't see and she can't talk and she is scared. We walk around the hall. I get her in her chair and I push her in circles around the unit.

When I leave she is asleep and I smell like my mother's blood.

SOMETIMES IT'S MONDAY and you wake up with dread in your throat and you're thankful it's a school lunch your kids will eat and you can't find their folders and it's Monday and it's raining but you make the bus and after you feel like giving up so you call a friend and it's Monday. She meets you for coffee and you haven't seen her since Friday and not last Friday and you talk and talk and it all feels better so you go home to Monday and make the calls you don't want to make like the vet 'cause your cat has cancer and the tumor is growing into her eye and the pediatrician because your kid has fluid in his left ear and the insurance company because they made the check out wrong and now you are short nine hundred dollars and you call the editor of the local paper because they pissed you off and you leave a message because it is Monday morning. And you go to the vet and the cat bleeds all over everything and you ask when is the right time and they don't tell you and you pay a hundred bucks and then you come home to drop off the cat and go to Marshalls to buy socks to bring to your Mom and when you get there she is crying she is always crying every Monday. And you feed her fatty pot roast and mashed potatoes until she won't open her mouth and you walk with her around and around and Fred the Eugene O'Neill scholar who taught your friends sits in the hall and he calls Olive a bothersome bitch and she is so you laugh and you sing to your mother yoursing songs she sang to you and you sing Little Boxes. Little boxes on the hillside and they're all made out of ticky-tacky and Fred sings along and he claps his hands and he bangs his tray for the first time and they're all made just the same. You leave right at two to get the kids to bring him to the doctor and you talk to the school nurse about how stupid a stupid book was and the kids come down the hall in their raincoats and into the car and to the doctor's where they don't see fluid and your son fails a hearing test in his left ear but he gets a sticker and you go home and pick all the girly clothes from your daughter's dresser to be passed along because she isn't girly anymore and you start to make dinner and you burn it and your daughter spills her milk and the whole thing is a mess of messes until the kids go up to bed and you take a quick bath shave your legs don't wash your hair clean the sink and go upstairs. You hang up the clothes on the foot of the bed pick a dress for tonight and shoes heels and a sweater make the kids' lunches and leave. Monday night now bar filling friends and musicians and kids young enough you don't care what they think and beer tonight knitting out and a book to return and someone says they wish they had a washboard and you have one in the car so you get it and he plays it with your keys the old washboard from a friend's garage and you buy drinks and stand up because it is Monday and you are tired and the kids get up to play The Weight and Fisherman's Blues and you decide not to sit down more beer and dancing with the girls and at the end they play songs for you dirty rock and roll and your friend plays the washboard and sings Bowie and you dance til you notice your feet hurt and you remember working ten hours tomorrow on the same feet and you slow. It is Tuesday now, Tuesday. And Monday was alright.

TUESDAY, APRIL 24

MONDAY MORNING COMING down: bills paid, laundry in, broth on. Trying to catch up. Calls that need to be made: doctor, dentist, electric, gas. Food in the fridge needs to be cooked. Vegetables to be dealt with. Green tomatoes to gather.

Last night I dreamt I was going through my mother's possessions with my sister. Sorting through boxes to find the things that mattered. An ironstone cup. A scrap of fabric from a child's dress. This morning I woke up exhausted.

Today I have lists of things to do. None of them seem to matter. Everything I finish leaves me with a feeling of loss.

MONDAY, OCTOBER 22

2013

S UNDAY AFTERNOON, BACK aching from coughing all night. Shoulders sore, body tired. If I had television I could watch football all day and nobody would think ill of me. Instead I wander around the house trying to find something small to do.

Make soup. Knit limes. It may be all I can muster.

EPG

TODAY MY MOTHER turns 64. There is a party with loud nurses and children and neighbors with flowers. Balloons and slices of ham. A bottle of port.

They poke her and tell her to smile. Ask her if she is awake. Feed her sliced ham. I take her inside. We are quiet.

The man who lives in the house I grew up in comes with his guitar. He sings for her. He sings songs everyone wants to sing in a way no-one can sing along. Songs about mountains. Songs about trains. Will you still need me. Will you still feed me. She leans against me as he plays. She keeps her eyes closed. I hold a glass of port in my right hand, her hand in the other.

The man finishes his songs. The people start to leave with their loud goodbyes and their loud affections. I hold her and sing her a song as everyone turns away. She wraps her legs around mine and curls into me when I sing. It's by far the hardest thing. Follow me. I tell her I love her and leave.

The grass along the extension is purply-red. There are beans in my mother's pot. Yellow finches in the sunflowers. This summer will end if we wait it out.

Don't think twice. It's alright.

WEDNESDAY, AUGUST 21

2014

I DREAMED ABOUT my mother last night. This happens when I haven't seen her for a while. If I were a different person I would call it a visitation. That's what it felt like: a visit. She wasn't well but she was better, like the her of a few years ago. She knew who I was. We walked through roads around the water. She smiled at me. We said some words, not many. There weren't many to say. We were together, smiling in the sunlight, finding comfort in each other's company.

But this isn't how it was a few years ago. This is the part I sometimes put out of my mind. Her running from me, hitting me, biting me, calling me names. Screaming at the top of her lungs. Me sitting around the corner, out of her sight, so she wouldn't see me and turn to rage.

Thursday at the Farmer's Market one of the women who takes care of my mother held a picture of her in my face. She told me she was doing better, gaining weight. She was guiltmongering. Like she knew the story. Like she knew who my mother was.

SATURDAY, JULY 19

2015

THE CATS ARE curled up on the radiator. The kitchen floor still needs to be mopped. My feet are tired and my back is tired but my eyes are wide open. For the moment everything is quiet and I am happy being quiet.

THURSDAY, JANUARY 1

RAINY SUNDAY, WARM and wet. Yesterday's snow is all but gone. All around town people are readying themselves for tomorrow's routine. The market full of mothers buying food for lunches. Lines of cars at gas stations. All of us quickening.

It is nearly midnight. The kids have been in bed for four hours and still aren't asleep. They are fighting the end of the break tooth and nail, eyes wide open and bodies tense.

ALL OF A sudden the night isn't young. I forgo all that is left undone—the cleaning, the responding, the bills and the work so that years from now my daughter will remember me playing the fiddle downstairs while she was falling asleep.

TUESDAY, JANUARY 6

TWO AISLES IN and I find myself sad in Market Basket. I can't even make myself smile at the old people so I try not to make eye contact. Not even with the white-haired woman who lived with Danuta. I decide to skip much of the store. Get what we need for lunches and dinner. Look toward the end of the aisle. By frozen foods I am nearly crying.

I end up in the wrong check out lane. The woman ringing in my food smiles and jokes. I make a smile back at her. The boy bagging can't look up and can't start until he has all the food in front of him. He changes his mind about where the spinach goes. Lines the soda water up so the labels face the same way. I want to be home. The air outside is cold and full of memories. I want to be home where no one will talk to me. Where no one will remember him to me.

Outside, groceries in the back of the truck and the door won't close. Broken maybe from the cold or maybe from being old and tired. I drive home with one hand clutching the wheel, the other holding the door shut. On right turns it opens a crack and the alarm sounds until I can pull it closed again. On left turns I ease my grip. I make it through two rotaries, past a police officer and home.

THURSDAY, JANUARY 8

TODAY'S SNOW UNSHOVELED on the walk. Blankets hung in the windows. So much is going undone that eating leftovers feels productive.

TRY THESE ON, I say.

I won't wear these to school, she says.

The past week she has been tucking her long blond hair up under a cap and going to school as the new boy. She wears hand-me-downs from her cousins and pants from her brother's drawer. She calls herself Robert.

I know, I say. I didn't get them for you to wear to school.

She expected a fight. I'm not fighting. I unzip the brown leather boot and hold it out to her. She pulls the boot on and looks at me. I am not wearing these to school.

I got them for running with your bow and arrow, I say. Boots on, she leaves the room.

Hours later she is running through the living room, bow slung across her chest, long hair behind her, pink pants tucked into her brown leather boots. She is singing at the top of her lungs. I don't know what she is calling herself now.

T RYING FOR THE life of me to think of some words that ring true.

I T'S HARD, THESE days, to find a thing to say. I mean to find a thing to say that someone might say something back to. It's hard to have someone say something back. It is all too much.

Last night there were six drummers waiting to play. They each had their own style. One a little more uptight, another had jazzy flick of the wrist. One played earnestly. One without a care in the world. I was happy listening to each of them.

Today at the kitchen table we talked about words and poets and people. The sun was shining through the dirty window behind him. That window is my window, I thought. I am a housewife with dirty windows. I should clean that window, I thought. I know I won't.

I don't know what makes better words or better drummers or better poets or better people. I know what makes a window dirty. It is dirt on the window.

MY UNCLE BERNIE'S paintbrushes. A bobbin of yellow merino. A Moominpappa figurine.

I am dusting frames. I am sorting change. I am drinking too much coffee because I don't have your address.

2016

I USED TO have ideas. I remember having them. Thinking things, then putting them into words. Ideas that weren't connected to the people in front of me or the dishes or city politics. Ideas that came from other ideas or the sky or books or the way two shades of blue looked next to an empty box.

I told a lie yesterday. That losing my wallet was more of a hassle than having my identity stolen. The old lady at the party smiled at me because she had just lost her purse or it had been stolen and she was deep into getting everything sorted out. But I don't worry at all when I lose my wallet. And when my identity was stolen I thought about who I was and how little it had to do with my finances. And how much it did. And when all your money goes away it hardly matters where it goes.

SUNDAY, JANUARY 17

EVERYTHING IS HEARTBREAK today. The woman with the car doors open. The empty recycling bin.

There is a space somewhere under my rib cage. It is weary, aching, like a waiting room.

I lit a candle. Ate an orange. Wrote a poem on the wall.

Still it sits, still, that hollow, dreading being filled.

2017

T HERE IS A story I didn't tell you. It was years ago, not too many but a lifetime, really. My mother was in the nursing home. She couldn't sit still and she wasn't allowed to sit on the floor so I walked with her for hours around the locked dementia unit. We walked past her room, past the nurses' station, past the common room and the family visiting room. We walked in circles for hours, me holding her steady. She hadn't said words to me for some time but as we walked that day she said the same thing over and over again: Kill me.

Today on the radio a doctor was talking about patients at the end of life. About CPR and ventilators and feeding tubes. He told the story of a patient with dementia getting a feeding tube. In the middle of the process he said more clearly than anyone could have imagined those same words: Kill me. When the interviewer asked what he had done, he answered that they finished inserting the feeding tube like the family had asked.

That was five years ago. Today my mother lies in a hospital bed in the basement of her lover's house, carefully tended by women who don't know I am her daughter. For years I have felt like I let my mother down. I keep waiting for the story to end. I have done all I can.

MONDAY, JANUARY 30

NOTES

The drawings in this book are from a series of notebooks my mother, Carolyn Porter, gave me as she started to slip away, and from a series of sketches by my sister, Elizabeth Porter Grammas. The cover is a patchwork of my mother's drawing created by Ryan Gallagher who, incredibly, put the locust tree where it belonged next to the barn.

Many thanks to Joseph Torra, without whom this would never have become a book. Thank you James Cook and David Rich for finding what needed fixing. Thank you Stevens Brosnihan for helping with the images. And thank you Ryan Gallagher for making this book so lovely.

Six entries from Ironstone Whirligig were published previously in Poils: Resistance (Summer 2010).

Amanda Cook lives in Gloucester with her husband, James, and children, Abigail and Samuel. She sees writing as an integral part of life. She knits, spins yarn, plays fiddle, feeds people and dances when she pleases.

Author portrait by Abigail Cook.